ROVER SD1
1976-1986
OWNERS' AND BUYERS' GUIDE

by James L. Taylor

1991

Published and distributed by:
P4 Spares
60 Woodville Road
London NW11 9TN
(081-455 6992)

ISBN 1 873078 03 X

INTRODUCTION

The main purpose of this book is to help would-be owners of a Rover SD1 to choose the car which is right for them and right for their pockets. The model was produced in a bewilderingly large number of variants over the years, all of which had their good and their bad points.

The format chosen for this guide is a chronological one. The various models fall into groups, and each group is discussed in detail, with specification changes and other useful points. After each of these descriptive sections comes a detailed guide on the strengths and weaknesses of the cars. The advice it contains is designed not only to assist buyers in their choice of model, but also to warn them about potentially expensive faults. Because major items like engines are only dealt with once (on their first introduction), intending purchasers are advised to read *the whole book* and not just the section relating to the model of particular interest.

Also included is a representative selection of road tests, reproduced by kind permission of the publishers of *Autocar* and *Motor* magazines. Lastly, the book includes some helpful specification tables and, for interest, short sections on the development of the car and on SD1 "oddities".

Although neither the author nor the publisher can accept any liability for acts carried out on the advice given in this book, both would be pleased to be informed of any errors or omissions it contains.

Third edition (revised and enlarged)
January 1991
James L. Taylor

Originally published by the author as a *Character Car* guide.

First edition, 1986
Second, revised, edition, 1987
Reprinted, 1988

This edition, 1991

Also published by P4 Spares:

The Post-War Rover, P4 and P5, by James Taylor
Advertising Rover 1904-1964 by Daniel Young
Vintage Rover Anthology, 1920-1933, by Daniel Young
Sporting Rover Anthology, 1930-1968, by Daniel Young
Rover Anthology, 1934-1939, by Daniel Young
Rover Anthology, 1950-1967 (P4-P5), by Daniel Young
P3 Scrapbook, 1948-1949, by Daniel Young
Rover P6 Anthology, 1963-1977 (2000/2200), by Daniel Young
Rover P6B Anthology, 1968-1977 (3500/3500S), by Daniel Young

The Leyland Cars emblem.

The original "skeletal" SD1 badge.

THE ROVER MARQUE, 1970-1986

The period during which the Rover SD1 was produced was a very confused one for its manufacturers. When the car was first conceived at the beginning of the 1970s, the Rover Company was still a distinct manufacturing division within the British Leyland conglomerate. Within BL, however, Rover was in direct competition with Triumph in certain market areas; and in 1972, the two companies were formally combined within the Specialist Cars Division of British Leyland, where they made rather unhappy bedfellows with Jaguar. As a result of the Ryder Report's recommendations, BL's car manufacturing operations were centralised under Leyland Cars in November 1975, and thus Rover had become a marque within that manufacturing division when the SD1 was launched in 1976. From 1978, Rover was described as a division of Jaguar Rover Triumph Ltd, itself a 'member' of Leyland Cars. This remained the position until mid-1982, when what had been British Leyland became the Austin Rover Group. The company changed its name yet again - this time to Rover Group - in July 1986, when the SD1's successor was announced.

The 1979 and later bonnet badge.

The Austin Rover Group emblem.

DEVELOPMENT

The SD1 story can really be traced back to 1971, when British Leyland decided to initiate development of a new saloon car range to replace the Rover 2000/3500 models and the Triumph 2000/2500 cars. As the old Rover and Triumph companies were now part of the same division within BL, both were invited to submit new designs for consideration by the BL Board. Rover's "P10" design was preferred to Triumph's "Puma", and the selected model was renamed "RT1" (for Rover-Triumph number One) in reflection of the joint development work which would be put into it by the two sets of engineers. Within a few months, it was renamed yet again, as Rover and Triumph were absorbed into the new Specialist Cars Division. From then on, it was known as SD1, for Specialist Division number One (and *not* "SDI", as so many people mistakenly call it).

Almost the first thing which happened when P10 became RT1 was that Rover's plan to use a DOHC four-cylinder engine of 2.2 litres in the cheaper models was abandoned, and BL management decreed that radically redeveloped versions of the existing Triumph six-cylinder unit should be used instead. The top model, as originally planned for P10, would have the Rover 3.5-litre V8, an engine designed by General Motors in America during the 1950s but taken over by Rover in the mid-1960s and already a staple part of their range.

Two things were outstanding about the SD1. First, it was to use a hatchback body-style, which was a radical proposal for 1971 when hatchbacks were usually associated with small cars up to 1.5 litres and certainly not with 3.5-litre executive saloons. Second, SD1 was to be built to a price so that it could take on the best of the European imports.

Although dozens of designers became involved with the SD1 project over the next five years, it is worth mentioning the names of the key figures. In overall charge was Spen King, BL's Director of Engineering. Under him, Mike Lewis co-ordinated Design and Development, with Design being the responsibility of Gordon Bashford and Development being entrusted to Rex Marvin. Styling was carried out by David Bache. King, Bashford and Bache had all had long and distinguished careers with Rover, and had been involved with the design of the acclaimed Rover 2000 (P6) and Range Rover, among others.

The SD1 was built in a huge new factory on Rover's existing Solihull site, which was claimed to be one of the most modern in Europe and cost £27 million to build. Original plans were to build a plant with a capacity of 1500 cars a week, but British Leyland encouraged Rover to think big, and the eventual plant capacity was in fact twice that figure. SD1 assembly lines never filled the new factory, however. Closed in 1982 as a result of one of BL's many reorganistions (when SD1 production was transferred to Cowley), the plant has since been re-equipped for the production of Land Rovers and Range Rovers.

3500, 1976-1980

The Rover 3500 was launched on 30th June 1976 to ecstatic reviews. By the standards of the time, it was an extremely well-equipped vehicle, with class-leading performance and a price trimmed to keep it below £5000 and below that of likely rivals. Its aerodynamically-styled five-door body was strikingly individual at the time and, indeed, remains so fifteen years later.

The SD1 had conventional monocoque construction and, like many contemporaries, was designed with a rigid passenger cell with crushable front and rear ends for accident protection. Side-collision strength was aided by horizontal compression struts in the doors just below the windows, and the car had the new Triplex Ten/Twenty windscreen, with a toughened inner layer to reduce lacerations in an accident. This was bonded to the bodyshell to increase torsional stiffness. The body had been engineered in consultation with the Motor Insurance Repairs Association in an attempt to minimise repair costs, and considerable effort had gone into corrosion protection. The shell was electrophoretically primed and then sprayed with a new and tough thermoplastic paint, and the zinc-coated sills were ventilated to inhibit moisture build-up.

Despite an extra 7.1 inches in the wheelbase to give more rear legroom, the car was only 5 inches longer than its predecessor, and careful weight control had kept it down to 26.6cwt. The rear hatch lifted with the aid of gas struts to reveal a boot with a high sill which was only moderately-sized, but which could be enlarged in two ways. First, the rear seat folded forwards to increase the length and the parcel shelf lifted out to increase the depth; and then the false floor under which the spare wheel lived could be removed to reveal an additional well. A further increase in size could be obtained by mounting the spare wheel vertically. Estate-car carrying capacity was thus available within a stylish saloon.

Cost-paring was apparent in the interior, however, where the nylon velour upholstery was only available in three rather drab shades of brown. Injection-moulded plastic door trims and rear parcel shelf looked disappointingly cheap, and the instrument pod on the shapely dashboard - also injection-moulded - had too obviously been designed for easy installation in both left-hand-drive and right-hand-drive cars. There were interesting features, though. The inboard seat belt mountings were bolted to the seat frame, so that they maintained a constant position relative

to the passenger rather than the car. The thick-rimmed steering wheel was not round but flattened off at the bottom to give more thigh room, and the choke was a pull-up lever conveniently sited on the console beside the handbrake. The heating/ventilation system was the same excellent unit used in the Triumph TR7 and the Leyland Princess, with an air bleed into the doors for side-window demisting. However, it had no ram-air setting, so that the blower fan had to be on all the time if the windows were closed.

A welcome feature, rare at the time, was the central door locking system, while a twin-speaker push-button radio was also fitted. Green-tinted windows were standard, and the car came with a driver's door mirror which was adjustable from inside. The bumpers were of stainless steel with black plastic end caps, and wheel trims were also stainless steel, with black painted panelling in a "clover-leaf" pattern. Mudflaps were provided for all four wheels. Strip badges at the rear read "Rover" and "3500", while the bonnet bore a stainless steel Viking ship badge of a new skeletal design, which was repeated in the wheel centres. Twin fog lamps in the front undertray were standard.

The car's suspension followed Triumph practice at the front, with MacPherson struts and coil springs, and an anti-roll bar. At the rear, though, more cost-saving was apparent in the use of a live axle located by radius arms, a torque tube and a Watts linkage. Coil springs here were coupled with Boge Nivomat self-energising ride-levelling telescopic dampers, to maintain ride height and handling when the car was heavily laden. High-geared, power-assisted, rack and pinion steering was standard, giving a commendably small turning circle of 34 feet. Brakes were servo-assisted, with discs at the front and drums at the rear fed by a separate hydraulic circuit with pressure limiting valve. The standard pressed-steel wheels had 185 HR 14 radial tyres, but it was possible to order good-looking sculpted alloy wheels at extra cost, in which case the tyres were of 195/70 HR 14 low-profile type. A further option were Dunlop Denovo run-flat tyres on steel wheels identified by a red band around the rim.

The engine was Rover's twin-carburettor 3.5-litre V8, developed from its earlier applications to have a higher rev limit, improved valving, and more efficient exhaust arrangments. Its air intake also incorporated BL's award-winning air temperature control system for faster warm-up. With 155bhp at 5250rpm and 198 lbs/ft torque at 2500rpm, this power unit gave excellent performance with either the standard manual gearbox or the optional automatic. The latter was the same three-speed Borg Warner type 65 as had been used in the superseded Rover 3500, but the manual box was a completely new five-speed all-synchromesh unit. Although the 3.08:1 axle ratio and the internal gearbox ratios in the first four gears were identical to those in the old V8 Rover, the fifth gear provided an overdrive for fuel economy, which gave overall gearing of 28.8mph per 1000rpm and meant that the engine was turning at only 2300rpm at 70mph in top gear.

At the outset, the 3500 was very well received indeed, even though many owners of older Rovers found the lack of leather and wood disappointing. In January 1977, it was chosen for the Car of the Year award by a panel of European motoring journalists, and in 1978 it was voted Tow Car of the Year in Great Britain. Other accolades included the Don Safety Trophy, the AA Gold Medal, and the Style Auto award. UK Police Forces also bought large numbers for use as motorway and other patrol cars. Nevertheless, build quality for the first two years or so was very poor, and attracted a lot of bad publicity for the car.

Part of the problem was that the SD1 was being built by an inexperienced work-force, because Rover had been obliged to recruit massively when they opened the new assembly plant. Another difficulty was that it was being built very strictly down to a price, and this led to cost-cutting in vital areas such as quality control. The generally negative image which Leyland Cars had in the marketplace at that time was compounded by deficiencies such as these and, after a major oil price rise in 1979 made big-engined cars

temporarily unpopular, it was not surprising that SD1 sales failed to live up to expectations.

While struggling to get the build quality right, BL made a few small changes to the specification. When the six-cylinder SD1s arrived in October 1977, the 3500 was upgraded by the standardisation of a passenger door mirror, electric window lifts, and a four-speaker radio/cassette unit, all of which had previously been extra-cost options. A sliding steel sunroof became an extra-cost option in April 1978, and so did leather upholstery, though the latter was only available in a medium brown known as Nutmeg. In the middle of 1978, inertia-reel rear seat belts were standardised and metallic paint became a no-cost option, and then black paint became available at extra cost in February 1979.

Significant changes were made that summer, in the wake of the new V8-S model's arrival. A Borg Warner type 66 automatic gearbox replaced the earlier type 65, although the ratios remained as before. Alloy wheels of a slightly different pattern became available for use with the Denovo tyres and, like the Denovo steel wheels, bore a red band around the rim. Ordinary alloys became standard wear in November, and there were new rear badges with larger lettering describing the car as a "3500 V8", plus V8 badges on the front wings and a "traditional" Rover badge on the bonnet to replace the unloved skeletal one. Wheel centre emblems also changed to an outline of the traditional badge. Air conditioning became optional, and there was carpet material on the rear parcel shelf to stop items stowed there from sliding about. Finally, a headlamp wash/wipe also became optional and the PAS was improved with a new integral pump and reservoir.

An early 3500 with optional alloy wheels.

Wearing standard wheels, this car shows the pre-autumn 1979 rear badging.

The engine bay of an early V8 - in this case, a 1979 Italian-market V8-S.

The dashboard of an early 3500. This car, unusually, has manual window lifts.

Loadspace versiaility of the SD1. Very early cars had the single parcels shelf support strap as shown here; most had twin straps, however.

The later wheel centre badge.

The original 3500 wheel trims.

Denovo alloy wheels differed from the standard type, and the trims on Denovo steel wheels also differed from the regular production items.

BUYING AN EARLY 3500

Acclaimed though it was, the 3500 suffered from an embarrassingly large number of faults in its early years. Despite the elaborate precautions, the biggest of these was rust, which rapidly attacked the wheel arches at the front and, more especially, the rear, and affected the lower edge of the big hatchback, the area around the rear lights, the bottoms of the doors, and the body seams in general. The paintwork proved to be of disappointing quality, and Rover had to deal with large numbers of claims under warranty when stone-chips around the headlamps and on the front panel turned into rust-spots.

Build quality was also appalling in some cases. A particular fault related to the end-caps of the instrument pod: the left-hand one (covering the fuses) tended to fall off, and the right-hand one was often misaligned. The plastic skirts around the front seat bases broke very quickly, door trims and parcel shelves rattled, and the electric window lifts and central locking often gave trouble. The latter, incidentally, is always noisy in operation.

On the mechanical side, there were teething troubles with the electronic ignition, and the manual gearchange was often stiff and notchy in the lower gears. Rover later recommended the use of automatic transmission fluid to ease this problem. The rear suspension used several rubber bushes, and assembly errors here could contribute to a poor ride. Fortunately, by the time the 1980-season cars arrived in autumn 1979, build quality was improving, and cars with V-suffix registrations are generally better made than earlier examples.

The good news, though, is that the V8 engines are robust units, which should be good for at least 100,000 miles without major overhaul. Noise from the top end is to be expected in a high-mileage engine and may indicate a worn camshaft, but in a low-mileage example it will probably be caused by oil sludge blocking the valves in the hydraulic tappets which are designed to take up a certain amount of wear and keep the engine running quietly. This usually means that regular servicing has not been carried out: at this stage, Rover recommended an oil change every 6,000 miles.

A 3500 in good condition is a remarkably refined car, with plenty of performance available. The engine's high torque at low speed and the self-levelling rear suspension make it an excellent tow car, although it can be affected by side winds. The ride-levelling struts are expensive to replace, and many cars have been converted to use Koni or Spax adjustable dampers at the rear. The ride is always agitated at low speeds, but smooths out considerably as speed rises. Cornering should be very flat (and excessive roll indicates spring or damper trouble), but the live rear axle lets the car down at the limit, when the inside rear wheel will lift. Mid-bend bumps can also upset the SD1's composure and cause the rear end to hop sideways. All SD1s suffer from wind noise around the door mirrors, and the parcel shelf tends to rattle in high mileage examples. Many cars have dented rear bumpers, because rearward vision when reversing is poor!

The sliding sunroof introduced in 1978 is not common, and is usually accompanied by a vinyl roof covering. Air conditioning and the headlamp wash/wipe are rarities, and automatic transmission seems to have been more common than the supposedly standard five-speed manual box. The optional alloy wheels are very difficult to keep clean, but do not deteriorate badly. Denovo wheels and tyres of both types are effectively non-existent now, as Dunlop withdrew them from the market in the early 1980s after persistent troubles and offered owners replacement standard wheels and tyres. Some early SD1s on the market will be ex-Police cars: these will probably have very high mileages and may be fitted with the Minilite spoked alloy wheels which many Police Forces favoured in order to give better brake cooling. Some 3500s of this age have also been "updated" with features from later models (commonly the post-1982 spoiler and bumpers), which may disguise their age to the non-expert but cannot compensate for the cars' inherent weaknesses.

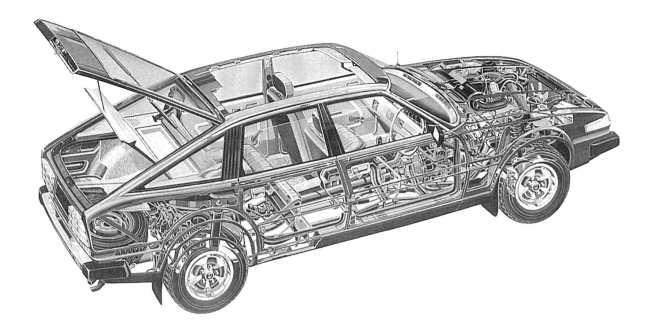

A cutaway view of the 3500 used in the early sales catalogues for the car.

This full-size cutaway car appeared at several motor shows.

2 3 0 0   A N D   2 6 0 0 ,   1 9 7 7 - 1 9 8 0

The 2300 and 2600 models were launched in October 1977, although the 2300 was not actually available in the showrooms until the following May. The earliest production examples of both cars therefore had S-suffix registrations. Although they shared the five-door body shell with the 3500, there were several differences in their running gear, specification levels, and appearance.

Both used variants of a new six-cylinder engine, the only components not common to the two being crankshaft and pistons. This engine had a cast-iron block and aluminium alloy cylinder head, a belt-driven overhead camshaft, and twin SU HS6 carburettors. In short-stroke 2300 form it offered 123bhp at 5000rpm and 134 lbs/ft of torque at 4000rpm from an actual displacement of 2350cc, while in 2600 form it had 136bhp at 5000rpm and 152 lbs/ft of torque at 3750rpm from 2597cc. Final drive gearing, at 3.45:1, was lower than in the 3500 to compensate for the less powerful engines. Although the 2600 came with the same five-speed gearbox as the 3500, the 2300 had a four-speed variant of the same design as standard, and the five-speed box was an extra-cost option. Both models were available with the Borg Warner 65 three-speed automatic transmission instead of a manual gearbox, and both could be specified with power-assisted steering if required. The 2600 shared the 3500's self-levelling rear suspension, but the 2300 had ordinary telescopic rear dampers with variable-rate coil springs.

Neither of the six-cylinder cars initially had tinted glass or front fog lamps, although both could be so equipped to order, and neither had central locking. Metallic paint, rear seat belts, and an upgraded radio/cassette player with four speakers were also extra-cost options. The 2300 had tungsten headlamps unless the other models' quartz-halogen units were specified, and it could not be had with the electric window lifts optional on the 2600 and 3500. Only a driver's door mirror was standard, and there were other cheapening features on these early 2300s: no glove-box lamps, passenger's map-reading lamp, or door-open lamps; different seat pleating and armrest coverings; no rev counter and fewer warning lights; rubber instead of carpet in the boot; and so on. It was usually easy to tell the six-cylinder cars

apart from the V8s. From 1977 to mid-1979, the 2600 had grey plastic wheel trims to the same design as the 3500, with blacked-out panels, while the 2300 simply had plain grey plastic trims, with black instead of chromed wheel nuts. Unless fitted optionally, mudflaps were not part of the original specification, and of course the badges at the rear told their own story. The six-cylinder cars had narrower 175 HR 14 tyres (steel braced on the 2600, textile on the 2300), although the picture could become complicated if the Denovo wheels and tyres were specified, as these were the same on all three models; and the 2600 but not the 2300 could have alloy wheels with low-profile tyres like the 3500. In practice, not many cars were fitted with any of these options.

Not many changes were made to the 2300 and 2600 in their first three years. Like the 3500, they could have leather upholstery at extra cost from April 1978, although very few indeed actually did so. Power steering was standardised on 2600 models in October 1978; and from February 1979, black paint became available at extra cost. The "1980-season" models saw more extensive changes, however. In line with the contemporary 3500 models, they had a coloured plastic bonnet badge and larger lettering on the rear strip badges. In addition, the 2300 now had the black-painted plastic wheel trims formerly fitted to the 2600, and the 2600 came with the stainless steel type which had earlier been exclusive to the 3500. Automatic transmissions changed over from the type 65 to the type 66, just as on 3500 models. Air conditioning became an option for the 2600 only, while both models could be fitted with a headlamp wash/wipe and alloy instead of steel wheels with Denovo tyres. Again, all these options were rare.

The slump in big-car sales which followed the fuel price increase in 1979 badly affected the six-cylinder SD1s. Stories were told of fields full of unsold cars, and many of the cars which had stood out for months in all weathers later became early victims of rust. Over the summer of 1980, the 2300 and 2600 models were discounted heavily in order to help dealers clear their stocks for the upgraded "1981-season" models. The last of these old-stock cars had V (and, in a few cases, W) registration suffixes.

Rear badging and grey plastic wheel trims distinguish this as a 2300.

The black panelled plastic wheel trims helped distinguish the early 2600 models.

The 2300 (left) had less comprehensive instrumentation, different seat trim and vinyl-trimmed armrests to distinguish it from the 2600 (right). Both cars here have 5-speed gearboxes and the 2600 has electric windows.

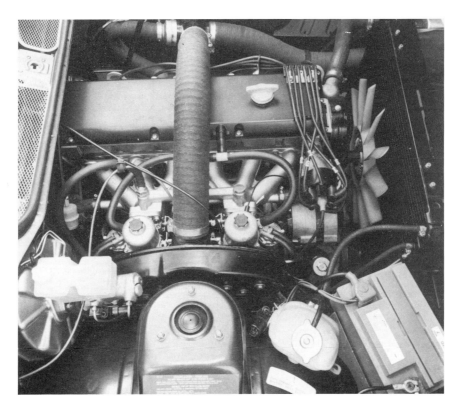

The underbonnet view of the six-cylinder engine was identical on the 2300 and 2600 models.

BUYING AN EARLY SIX-CYLINDER SD1

The 2300 and 2600 Rovers of this vintage suffer from exactly the same body-shell problems as the early 3500 models, and the faults caused by poor assembly are also the same. In addition, there are problems unique to the two six-cylinder engines.

When they were first put on the market, the six-cylinder power units suffered from high oil consumption (caused by oil seeping past the valve guides into the combustion chambers) and from burned piston crowns. These faults were rectified by Rover dealers under warranty, however, and there should not be any unmodified engines still around which are likely to suffer from these two problems.

However, both engines sometimes develop quite serious oil leaks from the rocker box cover, and both can become quite rattly if wear has caused the valve clearances to exceed the recommended tolerances. On an engine of uncertain or suspect history, it is advisable to get the camshaft drive-belt checked for signs of wear, as breakages are not unknown (and produce very expensive results). Cylinder head gaskets commonly fail at around 75,000 miles on six-cylinder engines of all ages and, if remedial attention is delayed, then more serious damage is likely to result. The spark plugs screw into tapered seats in the aluminium cylinder head and do not use a protective gasket: over-enthusiastic tightening can strip the threads in the plug holes, with the result that a plug will not seat correctly and the engine will misfire. Repair is expensive.

It was the 2600 which rapidly established itself as the customer favourite, and 2300 models have always been much rarer. 2300 models of this vintage are, frankly, too much of a stripped-out version of their bigger sisters to have much appeal. They were considered poor value when new, as compared to the 2600, and are still so today. The 2300 is not significantly more economical in everyday use, as its lower maximum torque generated higher up the rev range means that it has to spend longer in the lower gears; nor, in fact, are 5-speed manual versions that much more economical than 4-speed variants. Perhaps the only advantage of a 2300 is that some insurance companies put it into a cheaper category than the 2600 and 3500 models.

The 2600 is nearly as quick as a 3500, and far more economical. Significant performance differences are limited to acceleration at high speeds, although it must be said that the straight six is a less refined engine than the 3.5 litre V8. Most 2300 and 2600 models have manual gearboxes, although the automatic versions are not hard to find and are very pleasant cars to drive. The penalties of the automatic are in acceleration, maximum speed, and fuel consumption; the advantage, particularly in the 2300 model, is that the driver is relieved of the need to change down in order to maintain speed.

Like the 3500s, many six-cylinder Rovers of this vintage were fitted with vinyl roof coverings, particularly if they had the folding sunroof which many owners fitted because the steel sunroof was not available on 2300 and 2600 models. Although alloy wheels could be had on the 2600, not many cars were so fitted. The factory always fitted power steering with alloy wheels: some owners have fitted these wheels to cars without PAS, and the fatter tyres which go with them make the steering heavy at parking speeds.

Many of the early six-cylinder cars have already found their way on to the scrap heap, as second-hand prices fell very rapidly and the absence of luxury features on the "standard" models discouraged buyers at the cheap end of the market from buying a car which could be relatively expensive to run. Even good examples of the early 2300 and 2600 (which are most likely to be found among "1980-season" cars with V registration suffixes) can be bought cheaply today.

V8-S, 1979-1980

Despite their early policy of marketing the 3500 with relatively few luxury extras in order to keep its price down, Rover were not slow to recognise that there was significant customer interest in a higher-specification version. To satisfy this interest, the V8-S was introduced in June 1979, as part of the "1980-season" range revisions.

Mechancially, the V8-S was identical to the 3500, but in fact it was marginally slower due to the 340 lbs extra weight it carried, most of which was additional luxury equipment. It was also thirstier, especially if the air conditioning unit fitted as standard was used a lot, and the control panel for the ordinary heating/ventilating system was actually marked "Econ", to remind drivers that better fuel economy was available with the air conditoning switched off.

The air conditioning was a new unit designed by BL's SU Butec subsidiary, and fitted completely out of sight behind the dashboard. It had been designed primarily for the North American versions of the SD1, and was probably installed partly for "customer trials" purposes, so that any problems could be sorted out close to home before the US models went on sale in June 1980.

Leather upholstery was standard in the V8-S (though still only in Nutmeg brown), and cross-ribbed velvet a no-cost option. There were head restraints front and rear, with detachable cushions on the fronts, rear safety-belts, velour-trimmed door panels, brightwork highlights on facia and console, and shag-pile carpets. The sliding steel sunroof optional on ordinary 3500s was standard, along with a mono MW/LW radio/cassette unit and four speakers.

From outside, it was easy to recognise one of these substantially more expensive 3.5-litre models. Alloy wheels were standard, and on the first 900 cars were finished in gold except where Platinum body paint was specified or the no-cost option of Denovo alloy wheels and tyres was taken up. The windscreen had an indigo-tinted anti-glare band at the top, a headlamp wash/wipe was standard, and there was an extra cooling intake in the front panel for the air conditioning system. Other distinguishing features were black-finished bumpers, black rear badges, a twin coachline below the windows (seen on some export models from the beginning), and a bright finish for the exhaust tailpipe.

Black bumpers and the extra air intake helped to identify the V8-S models.

The V8-S had headlamp wipers as standard and special badging.

BUYING A V8-S

The V8-S is a fairly rare model and it is doubtful whether the original production target of 140 cars per week was ever attained. The very first examples had T registration suffixes, and a few of the last gained W-plates, but by far the majority had V-suffix numbers. This rarity value, the extra luxury features, and the generally improved build quality over earlier cars mean that the V8-S models command a price premium, both as compared to 3500 models of the same age and to earlier cars.

The extra luxury features certainly make this one of the more desirable early SD1s, although the increased fuel consumption may be a drawback to some buyers. The air conditioning is an effective and reliable unit, and although its value in the UK climate must be questionable, it does enhance the luxury appeal of the V8-S. Metallic paint was a no-cost option, and so a majority of V8-S models had it. As this was a car aimed high up the luxury market, most were also fitted with automatic transmission. The Denovo wheels and tyres were always rare, and surviving cars should all have been converted back to standard wheels. It is also very unlikely that any survivors will retain their chromed tailpipes, as owners generally preferred to fit the cheaper standard type when replacement became necessary.

Velvet upholstery and the rear headrests with detachable cushions in a V8-S.

Integrated heating, ventilation and air-conditioning controls in a V8-S.

2300, 2300S, 2600S, 3500SE AND VANDEN PLAS, 1980-1981

The "1980-season" SD1s showed that Rover were at last getting to grips with the car's lack of appointments and its poor build quality, and the "1981-season" models, introduced at the Motor Show in October 1980, demonstrated their determination to make the car worthy of the old Rover Company's tradition of excellence.

For 1981, there were five SD1 models in place of the previous four. As before, the bottom of the range car was a 2300, but above this came a better equipped version with the same engine, called a 2300S. The popular middle-range car was upgraded in specification to become a 2600S, and the mainstream 3.5-litre was now called the 3500SE while the heavily revised top model was known as the Vanden Plas. This name had never been previously used on a Rover, although it had been used on Daimlers and on badge-engineered Austins, and of course originally belonged to a coachworking concern which had been bought out by Austin in the late 1940s.

The most significant changes were to the interior of all models. There were four new colours - green, blue, light brown and dark brown - and the instrument pod surrounds were coloured to match the rest of the interiors. There were improved carpets (though the base 2300 still had rubber in the boot), plus a leather-bound steering wheel and a fully-carpeted rear parcels shelf. The seats themselves were now upholstered in velvet, with pinstriped central and plain outer panels, on all but the cheapest 2300 model (which had cropped velour upholstery in light or dark brown only) and the most expensive Vanden Plas (which had leather in light or dark brown as standard, and hairline woven velvet as a no-cost option). The front seats had an adjustable lumbar pad - though, again, not on the 2300 - and their reshaped backrests gave more legroom for rear passengers, who also benefitted from re-contoured rear seats to give them more headroom. Improved reclining mechanisms with a turnwheel control for the front seats also gave these a finer adjustment.

Although essentially similar to that on earlier SD1s, the switchgear was now illuminated at night and a long-standing criticism had been countered by the introduction of a ram-air setting for the heating/ventilating system. New kickplates on the door sills advertised the Rover name, and automatic models had a much improved selector lever with a neat push-button release in place of the old T-handle. There was extra sound deadening material on the floor and

under the bonnet, and the steel sunroof was now available on all models, and standard on the two V8s. Rear seat belts and a radio/cassette unit with four speakers were also standard on the V8 models, and optional on all the others.

The Vanden Plas did even better, with an electrically-operated sunroof, electrically adjusted and heated door mirrors, shag pile footwell overmats, four headrests (each with a detachable cushion), a cruise control, and the zone-tinted screen first seen on the V8-S. The V8-S style of bright trim on facia and console was also carried over for the new top model. Electric window lifts were standard on the 2600S and above, but the base-model 2300 still made do without even central locking.

Changes to the outside were less far-reaching, but new paint colours and bright housings for the door mirrors were a welcome revitalisation for the range, and all models now had the extra frontal air intake introduced on the V8-S. More important, however, was that bodies were now being painted at Cowley instead of Solihull, and the new process used there guaranteed much better quality.

There were many detail changes to the cars' appearance for 1981. The base-model 2300 gained a new style of silver plastic wheel trim with radial slots and a black centre, while the 2300S and 2600S shared the stainless steel 'clover leaf' trim, and the V8s came with alloys. On the Vanden Plas, these were machined and painted dark grey. Denovo wheels and tyres remained available, and were a no-cost option (with alloy wheels, of course) on both V8 models. There were additional identifying badges reading "2600" or "V8" on the front wings of all models with those engines. The Vanden Plas was readily recognised from the rear by black badges and the bright finish on its exhaust tailpipe; like the 3500SE, it also had a rubber strip on both front and rear bumpers, though its large front overriders containing washer jets for the headlamps cost extra if specified on other models. In addition, the Vanden Plas had black rubber bump-strips in the body-side indentations, and shared a V8-S-style twin coachline with the 3500SE. Tinted glass was also standard on the two V8 models, but only optional on all the others. Sadly, the expensive Ten/Twenty windscreen slipped quietly from the specification, to be replaced on all models by an ordinary laminated one.

There were very few mechanical changes. The four-speed gearbox remained standard on both

The interior of this 1981 3500SE shows the new pinstripe velvet upholstery and single-plane automatic transmision selecter lever.

2300 and 2300S models, and the base model 2300 came without the PAS standard on the 2300S. On the five-speed gearboxes, the ratio of the over-drive fifth was raised to give better fuel economy at cruising speeds, with the result that the V8 models became the highest-geared production cars in the world with an overall figure of 29.7mph per 1000rpm. This made no difference to maximum speeds, although the Vanden Plas, which had put on a further 165 lbs over the superseded V8-S, was now noticeably slower than the 3500SE. The only other changes were to the suspension, with more compliance at the front to reduce harshness in all models, and recalibrated rear self-levelling units with shorter coil springs to give a lower ride height and improved handling to the 2600S, 3500SE, and Vanden Plas.

The 1981 Vanden Plas had painted alloy wheels, a twin coachline, bump rubbers in the bodyside moulding and headlamp washers on the front bumper.

From the rear, badging made the Vanden Plas unmistakeable.

This 1981 2600S shows the larger lettering used on the rear badges since mid-1979. Just visible are the front wing badges, reading "2600".

The Unipart rear wash/wipe fitted to a 1981 Vanden Plas model.

BUYING A 1981-SEASON SD1

Without any doubt, these are the best of the early SD1s, combining higher specification levels with improved build standards. Quality was still not faultless, however, and though the new paint process ensured that the paint stayed on the cars to prevent the rapid rusting so common in earlier examples, there were still frequent cases of poor panel fit or electrical maladies. Nevertheless, the 1981-season cars are generally much more desirable than earlier SD1s. Their prices will reflect this, but will still be substantially lower than those of the post-"facelift" models. For buyers on a limited budget, these are the ones to go for.

The base-model 2300 is still something of a curate's egg, as it lacks so much of the equipment which makes the more up-market SD1s so attractive. Although some of this was available as options, most buyers who were prepared to spend a little extra went for the better-equipped 2300S. Manual boxes are definitely preferable on these smaller 'sixes': Rover's official fuel consumption figures show that an automatic 2300 or 2300S is actually less economical than an automatic 3.5 litre model! Problems with both the 2.3-litre and 2.6-litre engines had been all but eliminated by the time these cars were built, so there should be no worries on that score.

The most commonly available model will certainly be the 2600S, which represents a good buy. It has electric windows and a sunroof as standard, and both manual and automatic versions are likely to be readily available. 3500SE models are also reasonably plentiful, mostly fitted with automatic transmission as before, but the Vanden Plas is much harder to find. Its equipment levels and good looks do make it a desirable piece of property, and prices will of course reflect this. However, most cars will be automatics, which denies owners the benefit of the new long-legged gearing in the manual gearboxes and, together with the increased weight of the extra equipment, can contribute to disappointing fuel economy. Prospective buyers should remember that the Vanden Plas was never designed to be run on a limited budget. Two other points are worth bearing in mind: first, the electric sunroof is irritatingly slow in operation, and can fail; and second, the value of the rubber bump-strips in protecting the doors from minor knocks is questionable.

Many of the 1981-season 3500SE and Vanden Plas cars were fitted from new with a Unipart rear window wash/wipe system, which is a worthwhile addition. Tinted glass was standard only on V8 models, and was probably not specified very often as an option on the 2.3-litre cars, although there is a reasonable chance of finding a 2600S with it fitted. Alloy wheels are not very common on the 2600S of this vintage, and both the steel and alloy Denovos were rarely specified on any model in the range. Leather upholstery and the headlamp washers are almost non-existent on any cars except the Vanden Plas. Lastly, the bright exhaust tailpipe originally fitted to Vanden Plas models is likely to have disappeared as owners have fitted the cheaper 'standard' replacement.

2300, 2300S, 2600S, AND 3500 VANDEN PLAS
1982-1986
2600 SE AND 3500SE, 1982-1984
2600 VANDEN PLAS, 1984-1986

On 20th January 1982, Rover launched a facelifted SD1 range, which embraced the same five models as before, plus the new four-cylinder 2000 (dealt with separately here). The new cars were built at Cowley, to where the assembly lines had been transferred in December 1981, and benefitted from a mass of worthwhile improvements.

Styling changes made the 1982 models immediately recognisable. The headlamps were now flush with the bonnet panel, and a bright trim strip ran above them and along the lower edge of the bonnet, while a black plastic radiator air intake grille ran across the full width of the car. The sidelights were now incorporated in the headlamps (and the 2300 at last got quartz lamps as standard), and the front indicator lenses wrapped all the way round, like those introduced in 1980 for US-market cars. Beneath the new black polyurethane bumper with its increased wrap-around, all models except the new 2000 and the 2300 had a deformable plastic spoiler painted to match the body. The 2300S and above had bright trim on both front and rear bumpers, and all models had a new rear window, enlarged downwards for better visibility and equipped as standard with a wash/wipe system. A new full-width badge plinth also decorated the rear, with appropriate badging to distinguish one model from another.

The Vanden Plas model had a black side rubbing strip mounted below the body indentation, with a bright insert to continue the bumper line. Designed to be easier to clean than the earlier type, restyled alloy wheels were standard on the 3500SE and optional on other models, while on the Vanden Plas they had a machined and painted finish. The 2300S and 2600S gained stainless steel wheel trims of a new design, and on the two V8-engined models, a "3500" badge replaced the 1981-season "V8" badge on the front wings. Both V8 models also had a twin coachline. Bronze tinted glass was standard on the V8s and optional on lesser models and, as before, mudflaps and front foglamps were standard on these two models and optional elsewhere. The Vanden Plas had headlamp washers mounted in its front overriders, and these too could be ordered at extra cost on other models. All models had a new screen wash system with a vigorous fan-shaped spray, which was more effective at speed than the old type.

Although the upholstery remained essentially as before, 3500SE models now had the same hairline velvet trim as was optional on the Vanden Plas. Rover also claimed that head and legroom in the front had been increased, but the few millimetres extra made no discernible difference. A new and wider instrument binnacle greatly enhanced the interior appearance, while the steering wheel now bore a bright nameplate and the column stalks had swopped sides to meet ISO standards. Among the revised instruments was now a digital clock with an elapsed-time function, supplemented on Vanden Plas models by a multi-function trip computer which could be specified at extra cost on other models. Controls for clock and computer were sited on the revised console, which also had improved heater controls, a lidded trinket box (which was also ideal for storing cassettes in cars fitted with a cassette player), and a neater gear lever and gaiter for the manual-transmission cars. Door trims were better quality mouldings to a neater design, and on the S-models featured satin-finish wood inserts; on the 3500SE, the inserts were of burr walnut, while the Vanden Plas also had a burr walnut panel running across the facia. All models now had safety-belts colour-keyed to the interior, and all except the 2300 had central locking as standard, plus a sunroof (electrically operated in the Vanden Plas and optionally on others), and a maplight in the dashboard.

As before, the Vanden Plas had the plushest specification, improved now by the addition of map pockets behind the front seats and a three-band radio/cassette player. The 3500SE still had a two-band unit albeit with the four speakers and electric aerial also standard on the Vanden Plas. The 2600S and cheaper models came with only two speakers, but the additional pair could of course be fitted optionally. Both the V8s had a courtesy lamp delay, a second cigarette lighter in the rear, and rear seat reading lamps.

There had been mechanical improvements, too. All manual gearboxes now had five speeds, and all the six- and eight-cylinder engines had an automatic choke. The 2600S and both V8 models had recalibrated self-levelling struts to give a better controlled ride and tauter handling, and all models had a bigger brake servo for improved stopping and a new master cylinder for better pedal "feel". Pad wear sensors were also fitted to the front brakes of all models. The six-cylinder engines gained a remote air cleaner to cut down induction roar, while the V8s had stiffened cylinder blocks to reduce noise, and Solex instead of SU carburettors; these were said to improve fuel economy. Minor changes to the six-cylinder engines also resulted in improved fuel economy, and service intervals for all engines were now extended to 12,000 miles. A redesigned electrical system led to improved reliability and to more consistent operation of the central locking.

The range did not remain static for long. The 2400SD Turbo arrived in April 1982, and in October the new Vitesse was joined by the 2600SE variant. (Both 2400SD Turbo and Vitesse are dealt with separately). The 2600SE's specification was identical to that of the 3500SE except for the engine, and the absence of a courtesy lamp delay, rear cigarette lighter, electric aerial, and underbonnet lamps. October 1982 also saw bronze tinted glass standardised across the range and carpeted lower door kick panels with plastic speaker panels on SE models and above. During the 1983 model-year, GM 180 gearboxes replaced the Borg Warner type 66 on cars with automatic transmission; gear ratios were slightly altered, but made no discernible difference in driving. Motorised central locking replaced the solenoid type at about the same time.

There were some minor changes in July 1983, when Rover introduced a new range of trim colours, now commonised as far as possible in both colour and fabric with the rest of the Austin Rover range. The 2300 was given Shetland tweed upholstery fabric as standard, and the hairline velvet option on the Vanden Plas was replaced by Raschelle knitted fabric. Door trims now incorporated a contrasting colour as well as the main interior hue, and exterior door handles for the 1984 season had black plastic surrounds instead of the bright metal type used earlier. In addition, new air conditioning and cruise control systems were introduced for cars so equipped.

May 1984 saw a further series of revisions. Both 2600SE and 3500SE models were discontinued, and a new 2600 Vanden Plas variant arrived, with a specification like that of the 3500 Vanden Plas. The new top-of-the-range model was meanwhile the Vanden Plas EFi (which is discussed seperately). The 2300's Shetland tweed upholstery was replaced by the plain-and-pinstripe velevet formerly found in the S-model cars, and the car also gained the S-model wheel trims and wooden door fillets with electric window lifts and central locking, plus their programmed wash/wipe system. The S-models meanwhile gained the hairline velvet upholstery of the old SE models, and alloy wheels and automatic transmission as standard (though the five-speed manual remained optional). On all models, in-car entertainment systems were upgraded, the rear badges were mounted on the black plinth first seen on the Vitesse, and the shape of the door mirrors' base was changed to cut down wind noise.

October 1984 brought further changes for the S-models, which gained shadowstripe and plain velvet upholstery, and electric sunroofs as standard. The 2300, meanwhile, reverted to plain velvet, and box velvet became standard in the two Vanden Plas models while leather was relegated to an extra-cost option. Electrically-adjusted and -demisted door mirrors were standardised across the range, and the headlamps were wired through the ignition circuit so that they could not be left on by mistake when the car was parked. Both the six-cylinder engines and the V8 in the 3500SE were given SU HIF 44E carburettors with electronic mixture control systems to improve fuel economy. In July 1985, there were new colours and trims, and radio aerials were deleted from all models as the rear window demister element was wired in to substitute. Then from January 1986, repeater flashers were fitted to the front wings. July that year, however, saw the arrival of the first Rover 800s, and production of all SD1 variants came to an end, leaving 2300, 2600 Vanden Plas and Vitesse models available for a few months until stocks ran out.

The new "face" of the 1982 models is shown by this Vanden Plas 3500.

LOV 805 X was a left-hand-drive 1982 Vanden Plas press demonstrator.

A 1983 2300S, showing the wheel-trims introduced for both S-models in 1982.

Under the bonnet of a 1982 2600S, showing the relocated air cleaner.

The new dashboard introduced on 1982-season cars is seen here in a 3500SE.

This left-hand-drive 2600 Vanden Plas shows the leather seats of that model and the later type of two-toned door trims.

Post-1984 models had black badge plinths, as seen in this 2600S.

Post-1984 door mirrors (right) differed in shape from the earlier types (above).

The 1986-season front wing indicator repeaters.

BUYING A LATER SIX-CYLINDER OR CARBURETTED EIGHT-CYLINDER MODEL

With the arrival of the 1982 models, Rover were at last building the SD1 to the standards it deserved. The upgraded interiors, particularly in the 3500SE and Vanden Plas models, had an air of real luxury; and things got even better over the next few years as the luxury options gradually worked their way down through the range until even the lowly 2300 was vastly better-equipped than a late-1970s 3500.

Build quality of the cars from Cowley was also very much improved, and early rusting a thing of the past. Austin Rover (as the manufacturing group had been called since mid-1982) were confident enough to offer a six-year "Supershield" anti-corrosion warranty after July 1983. All of this is not to say that rust never breaks through, though: the join between the sill and the rear "wing" panel is always worth checking, and the front wheelarches may begin to show telltale bubbles after a few years. The edges of the sunroof are also prone to corrosion, particularly if the drain channels have become blocked.

Not everyone appreciated the new spoiler, and many people still fear that it might be easily damaged on kerbs and the like. In practice, it very rarely suffers damage, and is in any case of deformable plastic to withstand mild knocks. Nevertheless, some owners ordered their cars without the spoiler, and many Police models were so specified.

The raised fifth gear of the manual transmissions did make some difference to fuel economy at cruising speeds, but its benefit will obviously not be appreciated in town traffic. The popularity of the automatic transmission option was attested by its standardisation in May 1984 on all but the 2300, and this of course makes the more economical manual models harder to find. As with the earlier SD1s, most cars on the market, whether manual or automatic, will be 2.6-litre models.

Some of the options and luxury equipment are really not worth holding out for, however. The electric sunroof falls into this category, as do the headlamp washers; and the variations of in-car entertainment equipment can certainly be discounted when buying second-hand. The speakers fitted are in any case not of the highest quality and their performance will deteriorate with age, while it is very easy (and not too expensive when seen against the cost of the whole car) to upgrade the ICE system of any SD1. Denovo run-flat tyres were never offered on these models, although some cars used by the British Government did have the steel type with their accompanying plastic wheel trims.

2 0 0 0 , 1 9 8 2 - 1 9 8 6

The 2-litre version of the SD1 was introduced with the January 1982 facelifted range, and was a new base-model which gave Austin Rover a viable competitor in the growing 2-litre executive market alongside Ford, Citroen, Renault, and Mercedes-Benz.

The car's main novelty was its engine, which was the 1994cc overhead-camshaft 'O'-series four-cylinder already seen in the Morris Ital. In Rover form, however, it was uprated by means of twin carburettors to give 101bhp at 5250rpm and 120 lbs/ft of torque at 3250rpm. To overcome the poor power-to-weight ratio with this engine in the heavy SD1 body shell, a lower 3.9:1 final drive was fitted, giving overall gearing of 23.3mph per 1000rpm with the five-speed gearbox. The three-speed automatic transmission was also optionally available.

As the four-cylinder engine was considerably lighter than the sixes and V8s, softer spring and damper rates were specified at the front to maintain the cars handling qualities. Rear suspension was the same as on the 2300, with variable-rate coil springs instead of self-levelling, and tyres were 175 HR 14 size on 5.5J wheels. Alloy wheels could be ordered optionally, as could power-assisted steering.

Nevertheless, as the runt of the SD1 range, the 2000 initially lacked much of the equipment found on the more expensive models. Central locking, electric window lifts, a sunroof (either manually or electrically operated), and tinted glass were all options, and air conditioning was not available at all. In-car entertainment was the same two-speaker push-button radio as came with the 2300, although the four-speaker stereo radio/cassette could be had at extra cost. The headlamps were the quartz halogen type found on all other models in the range, but there was rubber trim in the boot and the seats were upholstered in plain velvet. The cost-paring process had affected the outside, too, and like the 2300, the 2000 had plastic wheel trims and no spoiler or bright trim on the bumpers.

Rover were soon under pressure to improve the 2000's specification, however, and from October 1982 both central locking and tinted glass were standardised. As on the 2300, Shetland tweed upholstery material was standard in cars built between July 1983 and May 1984, when plain velvet was once again specified. The May 1984 changes upgraded the car considerably, adding passenger grab handles and the adjustable lumbar supports for the front seats, walnut veneer door trim inserts, electric window lifts and a four-speaker stereo MW/LW radio/cassette unit to bring the 2000 into line with the more expensive SD1s. The external appearance was smartened up by the stainless steel wheel trims previously confined to the three 'S'-model cars, and the bright trim on the bumpers formerly fitted only to the 2300S and above. A black rear badge plinth, like that on the other models in the revised range, was also introduced.

A few improvements were held over until the Motor Show in October, when the 2000 was further upgraded with electrically adjusted and demisted door mirrors, a manually-operated sunroof, intermittent wash/wipe, and power-assisted steering. An electronic mixture control system was added to the carburettors, and electronic ignition arrived, together with the same linking of the headlamps through the ignition circuit seen on other SD1s at the time. That, however, was the end of significant changes to the 2000, and the only further specification changes came in July 1985, when new colours and trims arrived; in October 1985, when a three-band stereo radio/cassette unit was fitted along with the new aerial embedded in the rear window demister elements; and in January 1986 when the car gained the same wing-mounted repeater flashers as the other models in the range. The 2000 disappeared from the sales catalogues at the end of April 1986, to make way for the forthcoming 2-litre versions of the new Rover 800.

Wheel-trims, bumpers and badging distinguish this as a 1982 2000.

This later 2000 shows the black door handles introduced in 1984.

Under the bonnet of a left-hand-drive 2000.

BUYING A 2000

The 2000 was never a particularly popular variant of the SD1 , and prospective purchasers may have to hunt quite hard to find one with a specification which matches up to their ideal. Alloy wheels, for example, are a real rarity on this model, and air conditioning pretty well non-existent. The earliest cars had X and Y registration suffixes, most of the A-plated cars will have the Shetland tweed fabric seats, and the upgraded specification cars will have A, B-, or C-prefix numbers. A few cars may have attracted D-plates.

Although the 2000 started out as a fairly basic variant of the SD1, those built after May 1984 had a specification similar to that of the earlier bigger-engined cars, and are that much more desirable. The main drawback of 2000s of any age is their rather unrefined engines, which can sound very thrashy above 4500rpm or so. Although the overdrive fifth gear keeps noise levels down at cruising speeds, the engine does have to be revved hard to keep speeds up, and a lot of gear-changing is necessary in cut-and-thrust traffic. For this reason, and because of the low gearing necessary to give the car any sort of respectable performance, fuel economy is often not significantly better than that of the 2.3-litre models. Automatic transmissions *were* available, but were never numerous because they make the car slower, noisier at cruising speeds, and thirstier.

On the credit side, however, the 2000's performance is not as poor as might be imagined from its paper specification. The gearbox ratios are well-matched to the engine and final drive gearing, a top speed of over 100mph means that cruising at the legal maximum in Great Britain is fairly restful, and in fact mid-range acceleration is better than that of the 2.3-litre models.

Worth noting is that two batches of cars - dating from 1982 and 1984 - are said to have been built with the ventilated front disc brakes of the Vitesse. This was probably nothing more than a result of production-line shortages and, as there is nothing else special about these cars, they should not command a price premium.

2400SD TURBO, 1982-1985

In the UK, diesel engines and luxury cars have always been irreconcilable opposites, but motor and fuel taxation policies in some continental European countries make such cars a far more attractive proposition. During 1982, for example, diesel fuel in Italy cost only half as much as petrol. Austin Rover recognised that they could increase sales of the SD1 by offering a diesel engine option, and the result was the 2400SD Turbo.

This new model was launched at the Turin Motor Show in April 1982 appropriately, because its new engine was of Italian origin - and became available in UK showrooms in July. However, Rover never really expected to sell very many in this country, and only certain dealers were appointed to sell and service the car. Marketing was aimed mainly at fleet owners, as the only advantage of diesel fuel in the UK was mileage economy, and Rover believed that high-mileage operators would best appreciate this. However, the turbodiesel SD1 was offered with high equipment levels - it would always be on a par with the 2600S, with certain exceptions noted below - and it was priced mid-way between a 2600S and a 2600SE. Although the manufacturers claimed with justification that it was the fastest diesel saloon available in the UK at the time, they also admitted that savings in overall expenditure as compared to a petrol-engined SD1 were only likely to be realised after 25,000 miles.

Having no suitable diesel engines of their own available, and recognising that the potential sales of the diesel SD1 were unlikely to justify the capital investment needed to develop a new engine, Rover had decided to buy-in a power unit from an outside manufacturer. The one they chose was made by Stabilimenti Meccanici VM in Italy, and was known as the HR 492. A big four-cylinder with oversquare dimensions and displacing 2393cc, it had overhead valves and was fitted with a KKK exhaust-driven turbocharger with a maximum boost pressure of 10psi and a wastegated dump valve for overload protection. Fuel was supplied by a Bosch indirect-injection mechanical system to pre-combustion chambers in the four separate cylinder heads. As installed in the Rover, the HR492 was canted slightly backwards and had hydraulic front mountings to damp out the characteristic vibration of a diesel engine. Maximum power was 90bhp at a low 4000rpm, while the respectable torque figure of 142 lbs/ft was developed at only 2500rpm, which was lower down the rev range than any other SD1 engine except the V8 and helped to give the 2400SD Turbo a rather better performance than most people expected.

The engine was some 160 lbs heavier than the 2.6-litre 'six', and this and the extra underbonnet weight of the twin 12-volt batteries meant that front springs had to be stiffer. In fact, the whole car was heavy, weighing some 330 lbs more than a 2000, and so the 2000's low 3.9:1 axle ratio was employed to help acceleration figures. However, the diesel's limited rev range (it was red-lined at 4500rpm) would have given an unacceptably low maximum speed with this gearing and the standard five-speed gearbox, so the fifth gear ratio was raised. This gave overall gearing of 23.9mph per 1000rpm, good cruising fuel economy, and a maximum speed of just over 100mph.

Throughout its production life, the 2400SD Turbo received the same improvements as the 2600S, although there was obviously no electronic mixture control system among the October 1984 revisions, and the trip computer and automatic transmission were never made available. In fact, the only way of distinguishing visually between a 2400SD Turbo and a 2600S was by the badging. The turbodiesel wore "SD Turbo" on its rear panel, and "2400" on its lower front wings; but nowhere was there any acknowledgement that it was diesel-powered! The turbodiesel SD1 was last advertised in the UK in October 1985, and disappeared from the showrooms shortly afterwards.

The VM engine under the bonnet of a 2400SD Turbo.

There was no mistaking a 2400SD Turbo from the rear.

BUYING A 2400SD TURBO

Not many examples of the 2400SD Turbo were ever sold in the UK. The fact that they can only be serviced by certain dealers is a potential drawback to ownership, and intending buyers should first check whether their local Rover agent is able to work on the car. Although major service intervals are at the same 12,000 mile intervals as other SD1s, the irritatingly frequent oil changes after every 3,000 miles are a further drawback.

The diesel SD1 has a very different character from the petrol models, and demands a different driving technique. In order to get the best from the car, it is necessary to keep the engine revs up, changing gear with the accelerator pedal depressed beyond the mid-point of its travel both to maintain speed and to avoid clonks and jerks in the driveline. It is not the SD1 to go for if silence and performance are important criteria. Although the engine note is a muted hum at high speeds, cruising speeds seem to coincide with a period of resonance (though this differs from one car to another), and the distinctive diesel clatter is clearly audible at low engine speeds. Quick though it may be for a diesel, it is lethargic by the standards of other SD1 models.

Nevertheless, the engine is actually very refined for a big four and a diesel at that. The turbocharger is nicely matched to it so that there is no sudden surge as the boost comes in: all that is noticeable is better throttle response above 2000rpm. Starting from cold is rapid, thanks to quick-acting glow-plugs. The HR492 is a rugged and very understressed unit, which took the upgrading to 112bhp for the Range Rover Turbo D without showing signs of problems. Its separate cylinder heads are an ingenious piece of design which not only saved manufacturing costs but also eliminated head and gasket distortion problems. A faint whistle from the turbocharger is quite normal and need not cause concern. Fuel economy is astonishingly good for such a big car, especially in long-distance cruising, and works out overall at around 25% better than a four- or six-cylinder petrol SD1. When compared to the 2000, even acceleration does not seem too bad, for the 2400SD Turbo is more sprightly in both fourth and fifth gears thanks to its greater torque, and also has a higher top speed.

At present, prices are holding as well as those of petrol models of the same age, but it is difficult to predict what may happen in the longer term. Certainly, the 2400SD Turbo is never likely to retain a "rarity-value" price in its old age in the way that a V8-S may. Perhaps its future will depend on the success or otherwise of the new Rover 825D saloon, which uses an uprated 2.5-litre version of the same engine: if that sells well, it may help to improve the desirability of the turbodiesel SD1 and keep its resale value up.

VITESSE, 1982-1986

The high-performance Vitesse version of the SD1 was introduced in October 1982, a launch timed to coincide with that of another go-faster model from Austin Rover - the MG Metro Turbo. Designed to capitalise on the 3500's successes on the race-tracks and to enhance Rover's high-performance image, it was always to be a low-volume model and would only be available through certain Austin Rover dealers.

The Vitesse certainly looked the part. Its body shell was unaltered, but the car was shod with 205/60 VR 15 Pirelli P6 tyres on special spoked alloy wheels wth 6.5 inch rims, and sat an inch lower than the other SD1s on its revised suspension. A huge black polyurethane spoiler on the hatchback improved high-speed handling, and there were "Vitesse" decals along the lower flanks. To complete the picture, there were black fairings ahead of the rear wheel arches, the rear badge plinth was in black instead of aluminium finish, and the car came in a range of specially chosen colours. The alterations lowered the drag coefficient from the 0.39/0.40 of the standard cars to a useful 0.36 - not class-leading, but a very worthwhile improvement.

Inside, there were special "sports" front seats giving better lateral location, and the upholstery was in sculpted and plain two-tone grey velvet with no options. Satin-finish walnut trim adorned the door panels and facia, while the four-speaker stereo radio/cassette unit and trip computer were standard. There was a zone-tinted windscreen; air conditioning was optional; and only the five-speed manual transmission could be had. Up-market features included Vanden Plas-type headlamp power wash and electrically adjusted and demisted door mirrors, but the standard sunroof was manually operated, with an electric one optional. Rear seat belts were a standard fitment.

The heart of the new model, however, was its 190bhp V8 engine, uprated from the standard 155bhp tune through a higher compression ratio of 9.75:1, improved gas flow from reshaped valves with modified stems, and fuel injection instead of carburettors. The cooling system was also uprated to cope with the additional stresses on the engine. Torque was up to 220 lbs/ft, generated at a much higher 4000rpm, but its wide spread meant that tractability in the lower gears did not suffer as compared to the carburetted cars.

The fuel injection was the Lucas 'L' system, which had actually been used since 1980 in 3500 models for markets with strict emissions-control regulations, such as the USA, Australia, and Japan. In fact, the concept of the Vitesse dated back to the same period, though at that time it was going to be called the Rapide. When Aston Martin-Lagonda proved unwilling to part with their right to that name, "Vitesse" was dredged out of Triumph's past.

The export 3500s had of course been nowhere near as powerful as the Vitesse, where the fuel injection was tuned for speed rather than control of exhaust emissions, and gearbox, suspension, and braking improvements were introduced to cope with the new car's higher performance. The gearbox had stronger bearings and shot-peened gears like those used in the version fitted to Jaguars in order to withstand the higher torque of the engine. Spring and damper rates were increased by around 20% front and rear, and the self-levelling struts were uprated and combined for the first time with variable-rate coil springs. Stiffer bushes on the Watts linkage gave firmer axle location, and the front brakes were changed to ventilated discs with four-pot calipers, following the use of these components first on the racing 3500s and later on Police-model SD1s.

Not everyone liked the ostentatious decals on the car's flanks, and by the beginning of 1983 the Vitesse could be ordered without them. Some buyers, probably seeking the Vitesse because it was the most expensive SD1 rather than for its high performance, demanded automatic transmission, and so this was introduced as a no-cost option in January 1984. A year later, however, the automatic box was deleted from the options list, presumably because potential customers were turning instead to the Vanden Plas EFi model. Meanwhile, burr walnut replaced the satin-finish wood trim as part of the May 1984 revisions, and October 1984 saw the arrival of the Vanden Plas bump-rubbers on the flanks as standard, plus a redesigned front spoiler, unique to the Vitesse and developed from the racing versions. Its shape left no room for the previously standard fog lamps, and so these were deleted from the specification along with the side decals and wheel arch fairings.

In order to allow the racing Vitesses to remain competitive, Rover sought assistance from Lotus in developing a more powerful production engine. The intention was to build only the minimum 500 necessary to satisfy the racing regulations. The modifications made were to the injection system, which incorporated a twin-throttle plenum chamber, and to the camshaft. In production trim, 220bhp was expected. However, the racing camshaft made

The original Vitesse with side decals and rear wheelarch fairings

the cars less tractable and, as racing regulations permitted modified camshafts, it was omitted from the eventual production specification. The "twin-throttle plenum" Vitesses became available late in 1985; torque delivery was improved over standard, giving faster through-the-gears acceleration and improved response, but maximum power was still quoted as 190bhp. There is some dispute over the numbers of these twin-throttle plenum cars built; some sources suggest that the full 500 were never made and in fact no more than 200 were built.

The Vitesse remained among the three SD1 variants still available after the July 1986 launch of the Rover 800 models, otherwise altered from its earlier specification only in the use of the rear window demister as a radio aerial (from October 1985) and the addition of side repeater flashers (from January 1986).

The Vitesse always had a black rear badge plinth. This is a 1984 automatic transmission car, but there was no way of telling it from 5-speed models.

The 1985 Vitesse had a deeper front spoiler, side bump strips, no decals and no fairings ahead of the rear wheel arches.

Earlier Vitesse models had straight-grain wood veneer; this 1985 model had burr walnut.

Under the bonnet of a Vitesse. The later twin-throttle plenum models had two intakes in the cast plenum chamber.

BUYING A VITESSE

If the main attractions of buying a Rover SD1 are performance and its associated image, then the Vitesse is the model to go for. It has a genuine 135mph top speed, and its 0-60mph time of 7.1 seconds is faster than that of the legendary Ferrari Dino, as its makers proudly advertised during 1982. Such performance inevitably means a higher insurance premium, but the efficiency of the fuel injection system means that the car can actually be more economical than a carburetted 3500 - unless, of course, the full performance is regularly used. The Vitesse is a delightfully refined performance car, just as tractable at low speeds as the carburettor models but offering really strong acceleration, especially in the mid-range, and a pleasantly throaty exhaust note to go with it.

There are drawbacks, however. The fuel injection system in some early cars was unreliable, although later ones were satisfactory. The stiffer springing also means that cornering power may be up but ride comfort is definitely down, and the Vitesse's ride does not smooth out at speed in the way that of the other SD1s does. Tyres, though hard-wearing, are expensive, and of course not every Rover dealer is equipped to service the car. Whereas the DIY enthusiast can work on the carburetted V8, there is nothing he can do to the fuel injection without the proper diagnostic equipment.

The Vitesse has already been identified as one of those cars which in years to come will attain "classic" status, and resale values so far reflect its desirability. The twin-plenum injection models command especially high prices, mainly on account of their rarity. On the other side of the coin, the rather uncharacteristic automatic-transmission versions sold during 1984 are likely to lose value more rapidly than the manual versions. Neither cheap to buy nor cheap to run, the Vitesse nevertheless represents an attractive purchase to those who need its hatchback practicality and seek its performance.

VANDEN PLAS EFI, 1984-1986

Once the Vitesse had arrived, it was probably inevitable that there would be customer demand for the fuel-injected engine with the Vanden Plas specification, and indeed Austin Rover's Chairman Harold Musgrove was driving around in such a car by the beginning of 1983. The Vanden Plas EFi, with the Vitesse engine, suspension, and brakes in the fully-equipped Vanden Plas body shell arrived in May 1984.

Unlike the Vitesse, the Vanden Plas EFi (the letters stand for Electronic Fuel Injection) came only with automatic transmission, so that maximum speed was down by about 5mph and the 0-60mph time up to 8.2 seconds. This was nevertheless better than the acceleration times of a manual 3500 with the carburetted engine, despite the extra weight of the Vanden Plas EFi. Mid-range urge was of course also improved. From the outside, the car was recognisable by its Vitesse-style alloy wheels allied to an otherwise Vanden Plas specification, while of course the rear badging read "Vanden Plas EFi". This top-model Rover retained its original type of front spoiler after the Vitesse models had theirs reshaped in 1985.

Leather upholstery was standard (it had been relegated to an option on the ordinary Vanden Plas models), and box velvet an option. So fully equipped was the new model, however, that the only other option available for it was air conditioning. Not surprisingly, its cost price was at the same elevated level as its specification, and it was always a low-volume variant built to special order. Production ceased in spring 1986 to make way for the 800-series Sterling model which was launched in July.

Special badging helped to distinguish the Vanden Plas EFi models.

BUYING A VANDEN PLAS EFI

The Vanden Plas EFi represents the SD1 pinnacle in terms of luxury and equipment levels, although its automatic transmission may be a deterrent to some buyers. Performance is nonetheless exhilarating, especially for such a luxurious vehicle.

There are unlikely to be many Vanden Plas EFi models on the market at any one time, which will inevitably restrict choice for the determined buyer. This is less of a problem than with the lesser models, however, as there are almost no specification differences between cars (colour, upholstery material, and air conditioning being the variable factors).

Condition is therefore likely to play a correspondingly larger part in a decision to purchase.

The strengths and weaknesses of the EFi really combine those of the 3500 Vanden Plas and the Vitesse, in the same way that the car combines elements of both models. The fuel-injected engine can, of course, only be serviced by certain Rover dealers; insurance premiums will be in the Vitesse class; running costs will be high; but resale values are likely to remain buoyant after lesser models have started on the downward spiral.

EXPORT MODELS OF THE SD1

There were many minor variations on the home-market SD1 specifications for overseas territories, and not every model was available in every export market to which the SD1 was sold. Many of the variations were relatively insignificant: thus, for example, the 2000 sold in Italy had alloy wheels as standard. Others were curious and the result of local legislation: an example is the 1983 model-year Vitesse for Switzerland, which had a carburetted engine. However, there were three markets for which very special versions of the SD1 were produced. These were Australia, South Africa, and the USA.

Australia

The Australian market was only ever offered V8-powered models. The 3500 was introduced in August 1978, and had a "de-toxed" engine specifically designed to meet Australian regulations. With an 8.13:1 compression ratio and twin Zenith-Stromberg 175CD-SET carburettors, it put out 136bhp. The carburettors had automatic chokes (four years before the Solex automatic choke was fitted to home-market V8s); and emissions control was aided by an air injection pump driven by an auxiliary belt, an exhaust gas recirculation valve, and a charcoal canister which purged air from the carburettor float chambers and the fuel tank. All cars had automatic transmission. Alloy wheels and electric windows were standard, and many cars were fitted by Leyland Australia with an Alpinair air conditioning system. Controls and air ducts for this sytem were mounted on a raised panel in the centre of the facia, and additional ducting caused the deletion of the passenger side glove box light. Leyland Australia also added side intrusion bars in the doors to meet local design regulations, and split the brake warning light into separate footbrake and handbrake warning lights.

To stimulate customer interest, a small number of 5-speed cars were imported during 1980. These were fitted with the factory-installed SU Butec air conditioning system but were otherwise mechanically similar to the earlier Australian-market cars. In mid-1981, the 3500SE appeared. This was essentially a home-market "1981-season" car but with a 142bhp version of the US-market fuel-injected engine and badges reading "Fuel Injection" above the V8 badges on the front wings. Automatic transmission was again standard and, although 5-speed cars were offered for sale - with the 3.45 axle ratio of home-market six-cylinder models - in practice only 10 were imported.

The 1982-season facelifted 3500SE appeared at about the same time as its home market counterpart, and the Vanden Plas was introduced in 1983. Once again, the fuel injected engine was fitted although these later engines appear to be both smoother and more powerful than earlier types - a fact never admitted by the importers. Most had automatic transmission, although a small number of 5-speed 3500SE models - again with the 3.45 axle - were imported between 1982 and 1984. The SD1 was withdrawn from the Australian market when tighter emissions control requirements were introduced in January 1986; as its production life was now limited, Rover considered it uneconomic to adapt the engine further to met these new regulations.

(*Note:* This summary is based on material kindly provided by Rob Turner of Burradoo and Anthony Cope of Sydney).

South Africa

The SD1 models sold in South Africa were locally assembled from CKD kits, and had a number of idiosyncasies. Introduced during 1978, the range consisted of the SD (2600 with basic specification), SDX (2600 with high specification), SDE (3500 automatic) and SDS (3500 five-speed). Small details like the standard bump-strips along the bodysides distinguished these cars from home market models, and the rear plate badges incorporated additional information: thus, the SDX was badged as a "5-spd 2600", initially on silver plate badging like the home market type, but on black plates from mid-1979.

The main point of interest about the South African-built models, however, was that the six-cylinder cars had a locally-built 2,623cc OHC seven-bearing engine known as the R6 and derived from the Morris Marina four-cylinder type. This engine had a bore of 76.2mm, a stroke of 95.8mm, a compression ratio of 8.75:1 and produced 110bhp at 4750rpm and 148 lbs/ft at 2500rpm. Mated to a 3.7:1 final drive, it gave the car a maximum speed of around 101mph. Acceleration to 60mph from rest took 14 seconds.

The "facelifted" models were spearheaded in 1982 by the V8-powered Vanden Plas, but the other models were not updated until later in the year. They did not take on the all-black bumpers of the home-market cars, but had rubber-faced stainless steel bumpers, like those on the 1981-season home market V8 models.

USA

The North American market was offered a special version of the 3500 from June 1980. This had the Lucas L petrol injection system and an 8.13:1 compression ratio, together with a catalytic converter in the exhaust system. The engine was tuned for optimum control of exhaust emissions to meet the strict US regulations, and developed 133bhp (SAE nett) at 5000rpm and 165 lbs/ft at 3250rpm. The 5-speed manual gearbox was standard, the 3-speed automatic optional, and maximum speed of the manual car was 116mph, with a 0-60mph time of 10 seconds. The car was instantly recognisable from the outside by its protruding, impact-absorbing bumpers, its four round headlamps, and the Union Jack badge fitted to the lower edges of the front wings. There were no separate sidelights, and the front indicator lenses wrapped around in the same way as on post-1982 models; alloy wheels were a standard fitment. The trim and equipment levels were generally similar to the home market V8-S, with air conditioning and cross-ribbed velvet upholstery, velour-trimmed door panels and brightwork on the facia and console. Rear seat belts were standard but, unlike the V8-S, there were no rear headrests and a sunroof was optional. To suit US regulations, there were chimes to warn of unfastened safety belts and, to suit perceived US tastes, a special dished three-spoke steering wheel.

The car received enthusiastic reviews in the motoring press, but was let down by quality-control problems when it went on sale. Rover decided to withdraw from the US market altogether during 1981, after fewer than 1,000 examples of the car had been sold.

Huge bumpers and quad headlamps distinguish the US-market 3500.

Under the bonnet of the US-market fuel-injected 3500.

POLICE SPECIFICATION SD1S

The SD1, especially in V8-engined form, proved a popular patrol car with UK Police Forces, and was a particular favourite for motorway patrol duties. Many Forces fitted early cars with Minilite wheels in order to assist brake cooling; but the later alloy wheels did the job just as well and many "facelift" SD1s bought by Police Forces had them. Some Forces also removed the front spoilers. The 2600 was less popular, but was also purchased by a number of Forces for patrol duties. In 1985-1986, the Metropolitan Police took delivery of a batch of 3500 Vanden Plas models (presumably because Rover were anxious to dispose of stocks before the new 825 Sterling was introduced), but these were stripped of their Vanden Plas badging after members of the public complained that the Police were squandering money on luxurious patrol cars!

Many Police SD1s had cheaper specifications than standard. A typical Police-specification 3500SE would have had no sunroof, no central locking, no electric window lifts, no power assisted steering, and rubber matting in the boot. There would have been no bright trim on the bumpers and no headlamp washers. The gearbox would have been a specially-strengthened 5-speed, and there would have been alloy wheels and Vitesse-type four-piston calipers and ventilated front disc brakes.

A 1981 3500 in Metropolitan Police livery. Note the Minilite wheels with Rover centre badges.

A 1985 3500SE used by the Thames Valley Police for motorway patrol duties.

SPECIFICATIONS - HOME MARKET CARS

3500

Engine:
V8-cyl., 88.9mm x 71.1mm, 3,528cc OHV. Compression ratio 9.35:1. Five-bearing crankshaft; twin SU HIF6 carburettors (1982-1984: twin Solex 175CDEF carburettors; 1984-1986: twin SU HIF44E carburettors with electronic mixture control). 155bhp at 5250rpm; maximum torque 198 lbs/ft at 2500rpm.

Transmission:
5-speed manual gearbox; gear ratios 3.32:1, 2.08:1, 1.39:1, 1.00:1, 0.83:1 (1982 on: 0.79:1), reverse 3.43:1. Alternative 3-speed automatic transmission; gear ratios 2.39:1, 1.45:1, 1.00:1, reverse 2.09:1 (1983 on: 2.40:1, 1.48:1, 1.00:1, reverse 1.92:1). Automatic standard from May 1984. Final drive ratio 3.08:1.

Suspension, steering and brakes:
Independent front suspension with MacPherson struts, lower links and anti-roll bar. Rear axle with torque tube, trailing arms and Watts linkage; coil springs and self-energising ride-levelling damper struts. Power-assisted rack and pinion steering. Front disc brakes and drums at rear, with servo assistance.

Dimensions:
Wheelbase 110.8in. Front track 59in. Rear track 59in. Length 15ft 5in (1976-1981); 15ft 6in (1982 on); 15ft 7in (1982 on, with headlamp washers). Width 5ft 10in. Height 4ft 7in. Turning circle 34ft 5in.

2300

As 3500, except:
Engine:
6-cyl., 81mm x 76mm, 2,350cc OHC. Compression ratio 9.25:1. Four-bearing crankshaft; twin SU HS6 carburettors (1982 - 1984: twin HIF44; 1984-1986: twin HIF44E with electronic mixture control). 123bhp at 5000rpm; maximum torque 134 lbs/ft at 4000rpm.

Transmission:
4-speed manual gearbox standard, 1977-1981; gear ratios as for lower four ratios of 5-speed type. 5-speed manual transmission and 3-speed automatic optional. 4-speed gearbox not available after 1981. Final drive ratio 3.45:1.

Steering, suspension and brakes:
PAS optional. No self-levelling on the rear axle.

2600

As 3500, except:
Engine:
6-cyl., 81mm x 84mm, 2,597cc. Compression ratio 9.25:1. Four-bearing crankshaft; twin SU HS6 carburettors (1982-1984: twin HIF44; 1984-1986: twin HIF44E with electronic mixture control). 136bhp at 5000rpm; maximum torque 152 lbs/ft at 3750rpm.

Transmission:
Automatic standard from May 1984. Final drive ratio 3.45:1.

Steering, suspension and brakes:
PAS optional (1976-1978), then standard (1978 on).

2000

As 3500, except:
Engine:
4-cyl., 84.45mm x 71.1mm, 1,994cc. Compression ratio 9.0:1. Five-bearing crankshaft; twin SU HIF44 carburettors (1984 on: twin HIF44E with electronic mixture control). 101bhp at 5250rpm; maximum torque 120 lbs/ft at 3250rpm.

Transmission:
Final drive ratio 3.9:1.

Steering, suspension and brakes:
PAS optional. No self-levelling on the rear axle.

2400SD Turbo

As 3500, except:
Engine:
4-cyl., 92mm x 90mm, 2,393cc OHV indirect-injection diesel with KKK turbocharger. Compression ratio 21:1. Five-bearing crankshaft. 90bhp at 4000rpm; maximum torque 142 lbs/ft at 2500rpm.

Transmission:
No automatic transmission option. Fifth gear ratio in 5-speed box 0.77:1. Final drive ratio 3.9:1.

Pre-facelift and post-facelift SD1s together. The earlier car is a 1981 Vanden Plas; the later one is a 1982 2600S with optional side bump-strips.

Vitesse
As 3500, except:
Engine:
Lucas L type fuel injection; compression ratio 9.75:1. 190bhp at 5280rpm; maximum torque 220 lbs/ft at 4000rpm. Power and torque figures for 1986-model twin-throttle plenum engine not available.

Transmission:
5-speed gearbox standard: 3-speed automatic available only during 1984.

Suspension, steering and brakes:
Ventilated front disc brakes with four-piston calipers.

Vanden Plas EFi
As Vitesse, except:
Engine:
3-speed automatic only; no manual transmission option.

VEHICLE IDENTIFICATION

Number) of an SD1 will be found stamped on the scuttle panel next to the heater air intake below the windscreen on the right-hand-side of the car. 1981 and later models also have a plate bearing this number attached to the driver's door shut pillar.

SD1s were numbered in sequence from 000001, with some gaps. 1981 models began at 155001 and 1982 models began at 200001; Cowley-built vehicles started again at 250001. The last Solihull-built car was 215736 and the last Cowley-built car 345831.

This serial number is preceded by a series of letters which contain the manufacturer's own code and details of the specification. These codes changed in October 1980. As an example of an early code, the VIN number RRWVF7AA040882 (a 1978 home market 3500 with 5-speed gearbox) may be broken down thus:

RR   = Rover SD1
W   = body type (i.e. 5-door hatchback saloon)
V   = engine type (i.e. 3500 V8)
F   = model (i.e. 3500)
7   = steering and transmission (i.e. RHD, 5-speed manual)
A   = major model change code (always A on 1976-1980 cars)
A   = manufacturing plant (i.e. Solihull)
040882 = serial number.

An example of a later VIN number is SARRRHWM7CA211361 (a 1982 home market 2600S with 5-speed gearbox), and this breaks down as follows:

SAR   = world manufacturer code (i.e. Leyland Cars/Austin Rover)
RR   = Rover SD1
H   = model code (in this case an S-model)
W   = body type (i.e. 5-door hatchback saloon)
M   = engine type (i.e. 2600)
7   = steering and transmission (i.e. RHD, 5-speed manual)
C   = major model change code (C for post-facelift cars)
A   = manufacturing plant (i.e. Solihull)
211361 = serial number.

1976-1980 models						
	4-speed RHD	4-speed LHD	Automatic RHD	Automatic LHD	5-speed RHD	5-speed LHD
2300	RRWKA1AA	RRWKA2AA	RRWKA3AA	RRWKA4AA	RRWKA7AA	RRWKA8AA
2300	--	--	RRWMU3AA	RRWMU4AA	RRWMU7AA	RRWMU8AA
3500	--	--	RRWVF3AA	RRWVF4AA	RRWVF7AA	RRWVF8AA

1981-1986 models				
	Automatic RHD	Automatic LHD	5-speed RHD	5-speed LHD
2000	RRAWB3CA	RRAWB4CA	RRAWB7CA	RRAWB8CA
2300	RRAWK3CA	RRAWK4CA	RRAWK7CA	RRAWK8CA
2300S	RRHWK3CA	RRHWK4CA	RRHWK7CA	RRHWK8CA
2400 diesel	--	--	RRHWE7CA	RRHWE8CA
2600S	RRHWM3CA	RRHWM4CA	RRHWM7CA	RRHWM8CA
2600SE	RRFWM3CM	RRFWM4CM	RRFWM7CM	RRFWM8CM
2600 Vanden Plas	RRMWM3CM	RRMWM4CM	RRMWM7CM	RRMWM8CM
3500SE	RRFWV3CA	RRFWV4CA	RRFWV7CA	RRFWV8CA
3500 Vanden Plas	RRMWV3CA	RRMWV4CA	RRMWV7CA	RRMWV8CA
3500 VdP EFi	RRMWZ3CM	RRMWZ4CM	RRMWZ7CM	RRMWZ8CM
Vitesse	RREWZ3CM	RREWZ4CM	RREWZ7CM	RREWZ8CM

Notes:
1. The model change code for 1981-season cars was B (e.g. RRHWM3BA).
2. All models in the 1981-1986 table with VIN codes ending in A were also built at Cowley (when they had M as the final letter of the VIN code)

PRODUCTION FIGURES

2000	20,554	3500/3500SE/3500	
2300/2300S	42,996	Vanden Plas	107,916
2400SD Turbo	10,081	V8-S	1,040*
2600/2600S/2600SE		Vitesse	3,897
2600 Vanden Plas	108,572	Vanden Plas EFi	1,113

* V8-S figures for 1980 included in 3500 totals

No completely accurate production figures for the SD1 have yet been released by Rover Group; one problem in establishing these figures is that CKD production was counted differently at different times. The above figures are based on calculations made by Anders Clausager at BMIHT and refer to model-year (i.e. autumn to autumn).

These figures give a total of 296,169. This figure appears to include some, but not all, CKD vehicles, of which 14,376 were built between 1977 and 1983. Other figures from Rover Group sources suggest that the total SD1 production figure was either 303,345 (BMIHT estimate, inclusive of CKD) or 305,139 (exclusive of CKD and of a small number of bodyshells fitted out - probably for competition use - after production had ceased).

COLOUR CHART

	76	77	78	79	80	81	82	83	84	85	86
Black colours											
Black				79			82	83	84	85	86
Maraschino					80	81					
Blue colours											
Atlantis		77	78	79							
Azure Blue										85	86
Caribbean*		77									
Cavalry Blue					80	81					
Eclipse Blue								83	84	85	
Moonraker Blue*							82	83	84	85	86
Nightwatch Blue											86
Persian Aqua*			78	79	80	81					
Zircon Blue*							82	83	84	85	
Brown colours											
Aran Beige					80	81					
Brazilia	76	77	78	79							
Champagne Beige							82			85	86
Clove Brown								83	84	85	86
Gold colours											
Cashmere Gold*							82	83	84	85	86
Midas*	76	77	78	79							
Pharaoh Gold*					80	81					
Green Colours											
Avocado		77	78	79							
Opaline Green*							82	83	84	85	
Poseidon*			78	79							
Silk Green*										85	86
Sylvan Green*					80	81					
Triton*				79	80	81					
Red colours											
Bordeaux Red*					80	81					
Carnelian Red					80	81					
Monza Red							82	83	84		
Oporto Red*							82	83	84	85	86
Richelieu	76	77	78	79							
Targa Red										85	86
Silver colours											
Argent Silver*					80	81					
Platinum*	76	77	78	79							
Silver Leaf							82	83	84	85	86
White colours											
Arum White								83	84	85	
Ermine							82				
Pendelican	76	77	78	79	80	81					
White Diamond										85	86
Yellow colours											
Barley Yellow					80	81					
Turmeric	76	77	78	79							

Note: Vitesse models were available only in Monza Red, Targa Red, Black, Silver Leaf and Moonraker Blue.

The position on interior trim colours was very complicated. Thus, for example, the fact that Osprey leather was available with a certain exterior colour did not guarantee that Osprey cloth was also available with that colour. The following table gives a guide to the availability of colour combinations only, and does not refer to the fabrics used.

Black colours
Black
Nutmeg, Caviar, Coriander, Oatmeal, Osprey, Claret, Caramel
Maraschino
Caviar, Oatmeal, Prussian, Bayleaf

Blue colours
Atlantis
Caviar, Coriander
Azure Blue
Prussian, Ice Blue, Flint
Caribbean*
Caviar, Coriander
Cavalry Blue
Caviar, Oatmeal, Prussian
Eclipse Blue
Bounty Blue, Osprey
Moonraker Blue*
Oatmeal, Bounty Blue, Osprey, Prussian, Flint, Ice Blue
Nightwatch Blue
Prussian, Ice Blue, Flint
Persian Aqua
Caviar, Coriander, Oatmeal, Prussian
Zircon Blue*
Oatmeal, Prussian, Bounty Blue, Osprey, Brushwood

Brown colours
Aran Beige
Caviar, Oatmeal, Bayleaf
Brazilia
Coriander
Champagne Beige

Caviar, Bitter Chocolate
Clove Brown
Sandpiper, Brushwood, Caramel

Gold colours
Cashmere Gold*
Oatmeal, Caviar, Brushwood, Sandpiper, Bitter Chocolate
Midas*
Nutmeg, Caviar
Pharaoh Gold*
Caviar, Oatmeal

Green colours
Avocado
Nutmeg, Coriander
Opaline Green*
Bayleaf, Caviar, Brushwood, Osprey
Poseidon*
Nutmeg, Coriander
Silk Green*
Flint, Bitter Chocolate
Sylvan Green*
Caviar, Oatmeal, Bayleaf
Triton*
Nutmeg, Coriander

Red colours
Bordeaux Red*
Caviar, Oatmeal, Prussian
Carnelian Red
Caviar, Oatmeal, Prussian
Monza Red
Oatmeal, Sandpiper, Osprey, Brushwood

Oporto Red*
Oatmeal, Sandpiper, Claret, Brushwood, Osprey, Bitter Chocolate, Caramel
Richelieu
Caviar, Coriander
Targa Red
Flint, Caramel, Osprey

Silver colours
Argent Silver*
Caviar, Oatmeal, Prussian, Bayleaf
Platinum*
Nutmeg, Caviar
Silver Leaf*
Prussian, Osprey, Claret, Brushwood, Flint, Bitter Chocolate

White colours
Arum White
Brushwood, Osprey, Claret
Ermine
Caviar, Oatmeal, Bayleaf, Prussian
Pendelican
Nutmeg, Caviar, Bayleaf, Prussian, Oatmeal
White Diamond
Bitter Chocolate, Claret

Yellow colours
Barley Yellow
Caviar, Oatmeal
Turmeric
Caviar, Coriander

Notes:
1. All V8-S models had upholstery in Beige or Bronze.
2. All Vitesse models had upholstery in a combination of Flint and Osprey.

MISCELLANEA

* The last-of-line SD1 was made in July 1986 and was a Vitesse, finished in Silver Leaf. It was registered as D 537 PUK and handed over to the Heritage Collection.

* After production ended in 1986, the SD1 body tooling was shipped out to Standard Motor Products Ltd of Madras, India, where production had already begun in 1985 (using CKD kits) of the Standard 2000 - essentially an SD1 with a locally-designed gearbox, back axle, and 2-litre engine. This vehicle was sold only in India, where it represented the most prestigious of that country's domestic saloon cars. The original plan was for the Indian factory to produce replacement SD1 body panels for the Rover network worldwide as well; but production of the Standard 2000 was halted in 1989 and has not resumed.

* An estate version of the SD1 was considered for production right from the beginning. One of the pilot-build 3500 automatic cars was given an estate body in 1976, and at least one more 3500 automatic was built with the same type of body and registered early in 1977. A third car is said to have been built, and either this or the pilot-build 3500 was used by Sir Michael Edwardes for a time at the end of the 1970s. The second car, badged as a 3500E, seems to have been updated with 1980-81 paint and Vanden Plas trim, and was re-evaluated in 1982. These estate prototypes had a third, rearward-facing, row of seats. One is now preserved in the Heritage Collection; a second belongs to the Haynes Museum at Sparkville, Somerset.

* Several aftermarket specialists have offered conversions to make the SD1 go faster and handle better, and others have offered 'body kits' to make it look more distinctive. Performance conversions have included V8 engines enlarged to 3.9, 4.2, 4.4 and 4.5 litres, turbochargers for both the V8 and 2600 engines, and a variety of carburettor substitutions, extractor exhaust systems, and the like. Most of these performance conversions have been associated with the V8 engine; there have been very few to uprate the 2.6-litre six-cylinder, and none at all to uprate the 2.3-litre or 2-litre engines. In theory, it should be possible to fit the later 2.5-litre turbodiesel engine used in the Range Rover to a 2400SD Turbo, and this would put maximum power up from 90bhp to 119bhp and torque up to 209 lbs/ft at 1950rpm. Body kits have included front and rear spoilers, as well as more complete fibreglass transformations using bolt-on panels.

* The cheap-looking interior trim of the early models was a source of annoyance to some customers, and completely refitted passenger cabins using leather and wood were available at a high price from specialist converters like Wood and Pickett of London. Carawagon International marketed a limousine division in the late 1970s, though this remained rare. One firm also offered a cast metal Viking's head bonnet badge to replace the unpopular skeletal type on these early cars.

This car may have been one of the earliest of the estate prototypes; the known later example had some differences.

Among the styling kits offered was this one by Care Le Gant.

Steve Soper driving the Hepolite Glacier Vitesse, one of the cars which dominated the 1983 saloon racing season.

* The V8-engined models had a successful career in saloon car racing. The first 'factory' racers were prepared by David Price Racing in 1979, and preparation of the cars switched to Tom Walkinshaw Racing in 1981. The Vitesse became available during 1982 and ARG Motorsport subsequently scored a number of significant victories with these cars, which in racing trim produced around 300bhp. V8-engined cars also appeared in Rallysprint events during 1982. The works Vitesses dominated saloon car racing in 1983 and 1984, had a successful 1985 season and were still winning races in their final season the following year.

The Computervision-sponsored racing Vitesse, seen at Motor 100 in 1985.

PERFORMANCE FIGURES

The figures given here are those quoted in the manufacturer's promotional literature for 1985 models. They may differ slightly from those obtained by the motoring press in road tests, and from figures applicable to earlier models. In particular, everyday average fuel consumption figures are likely to be around 4mpg worse in most cases than those in the "Computed average mpg" column.

		Maximum speed	0-60 mph (secs)	30-50 mph in 4th	Computed average mpg
2000	Manual	104	12.7	10.1	33.5
	Automatic	101	14.1	--	32.1
2300	Manual (5-speed)	112	11.1	10.2	29.8
etc	Automatic	109	12.5	--	28.1'
2600	Manual	116	10.3	8.5	29.2
etc	Automatic	113	11.8	--	27.7
2400SD Turbo	Manual	102	14.9	8.7	42.8
3500	Manual	126	8.8	7.6	25.6
etc	Automatic	123	9.2	--	24.1
Vitesse	Manual	136	7.1	7.2	26.2
	Automatic	133	8.2	--	24.1
EFi	Automatic	130	8.2	--	22.8

Note: A collection of contemporary road tests and other articles relating to the V8-engined models only - "Rover 3500 and Vitesse, 1976-1986" - is available in the Brooklands Books series.

RoadTest

ROVER 3500 Automatic

The optional three-speed automatic transmission (replacing the manual five-speed unit) enhances rather than detracts from the overall excellence of the *'Car of the Year'*. Performance and economy are barely affected, and the rest of the virtues remain. Quality control not so good though: door sealing is poor and our test car suffered from a steering vibration

WHEN WE first tried a pre-production Rover 3500 we realised that Leyland were on to a winner. A much longer acquaintance with our long-term staff-cum-road-test car st▸ ▸thened this belief, although a gr▸ ▸ test indicated that we had perhaps under-estimated some of the opposition (the Renault 30 in particular). But nevertheless we still considered it a superb car. And now our opinions have been confirmed: no fewer than 49 eminent European journalists voted it 'Car of the year'.

One of the virtues of the earlier cars we drove was the delightful 5-speed manual gearbox, with its smooth, quick change and very high fifth (giving 28.6 mph/1000 rpm) for relaxed cruising at speed combined with astonishingly good fuel consumption. We were a little concerned that the optional three-speed automatic gearbox might adversely affect both the cruising ability and the consumption and thus spoil the car: having now covered a considerable mileage in an automatic version (we used it to transport four members of staff to Italy and back for the T▸ ▸ Show) we can happily report tl▸ ▸t is every bit as good as the manual version, for it is still a splendid long distance car, and the overall consumption (20.6 mpg) is still exceptional for such a capacious, fast, large car.

For this model Rover have simply swopped the five speed box for Borg Warner's model 65 three speed automatic unit, retaining the 3.08:1 rear axle ratio. Thus the 1.1 top gear gives 23.8 mph/1000 rpm, a figure identical to fourth on the manual box. In almost every other respect the car is the same: a five-door hatchback with a fold-down rear seat and extensive anti-corrosion treatment. The engine is the all-alloy 3.5-litre V-8 that produces 155 bhp (DIN) at 5250 rpm, and the rest of the specification includes Mac-Pherson strut front suspension, power-assisted rack and pinion steering and a well-located live rear axle with coil springs supplemented by Boge self-energising, self-levelling damper struts. It also means a lengthy list of standard luxuries such as adjustable steering, central door locking, and a remotely adjustable exterior mirror.

Our automatic test car was well and truly run in when we took it to MIRA, whereas the manual car was practically brand new: this fact may partly explain the excellent performance figures we obtained in comparison. It is slower, but only slightly: top speed is 120.0 instead of 122.3 mph, it took 9.6 sec to reach 60 mph instead of 8.9 sec, and the quarter mile times are almost identical — 17.1 sec for the manual, 17.2 for the automatic. So the alterations to the gearing have made very little difference to the performance on paper.

Subjectively, too, the performance feels as good, and the torque convertor removes one small gripe we have about the manual box — that first is too high, requiring more revs and clutch slip than you might expect for a brisk getaway. At or near peak revs the engine growls noticeably, but at all other times it is sweetly smooth and very quiet: 70 mph is a leisurely 2940 rpm (which compares with the 2450 rpm of the manual car at the same speed) and 100 mph corresponds to a subdued 4200 rpm (3490 rpm for the manual). Thus both cars are very long legged, and though the automatic does require more revs for a given speed the engine characteristics more than make up for it: we found on the Continent that the 3500 would cruise at between 90 mph and 100 mph so easily that slower running speeds seemed unnatural.

In spite of having two fewer gears than the manual version, we cannot fault the ratios of the automatic — they suit the engine characteristics admirably. For cross-country,

twisty roads or when overtaking we found that the ratios of the manual box tend if anything to be all too high — for brisk acceleration at about 40 to 60 mph it was necessary to change down to third or even second: kick-down of the automatic obviates this, and in this respect the automatic is almost better than the manual. The change itself under normal conditions was reasonably smooth, but it coud be quite jerky at full throttle and noticeably so on kickdown.

As with many automatic versions of a manual car, fuel consumption has suffered — but not very dramatically, and it remains very good for such a quick, spacious car, especially when compared to the opposition: only the W123 Mercedes 280E comes anywhere near with a 19.0 mpg overall as against the Rover's 20.6 mpg, and all the others are below 18 mpg. The touring consumption of 21.1 mpg gives a theoretical range of about 300 miles: in practice a non-linear fuel gauge and a warning light that cried wolf far too early meant that we were in fact topping up at 150 to 200 mile intervals, which is rather too frequent for long journeys.

We raved about the handling of the original road test car, and the considerable mileage we covered in the automatic version reaffirmed our assessment: even on twisty Alpine roads, covered in ice, it felt very safe, reassuring and predictable, while high speed stability is another good feature — both on the Autoroutes and Autostradas as well as MIRA's banking it was sure footed and stable. The adhesion of the Pirelli 185 HR 14 tyres was excellent at all times, and the power assistance to the steering gave just about the right weight and 'feel'. The brakes too work very well, slowing the car undramatically and quickly from high speed, but pedal feel could be improved, for under gentle pressure they are unprogressive and travel is long and spongey.

One of the reasons we chose the Rover for our trip to Turin was the

necessity to transport four people plus a week's luggage each plus camera equipment, and we could not have chosen better — all the baggage went into the boot very easily, and only a little judicious juggling of legroom between front and rear was necessary for real comfort. Should even more boot space be required the Denovo option is available, thus doing away with the spare wheel. Although there is theoretically a lot of oddment storage space inside it is less impressive in practice since any articles placed on the trays below the windscreen and rear window create distracting reflections in sunlight.

The Boge self-energising, self-levelling struts at the back proved their worth on this trip too, for even when fully loaded the 3500 rode on an even keel and neither ride nor handling seemed affected. However there was one flaw which was thrown into prominence on the concrete-block Autostradas — the cracks between the blocks caused a severe jolt to be transmitted to the interior as the back axle passed over them. Cobblestones, too, revealed a tendency to small-bump harshness.

None of the drivers or passengers complained of any discomfort, aches or pains even after a full 12 hours (food and petrol stops apart) on the road, and in general the seats were judged to be very comfortable. The front seats in particular drew praise, for their deep contours and plush velour-type nylon upholstery hold you in place, with plenty of the right support all around. The multi-adjustable seat and steering column means that a wide variety of differently-shaped people can find a near-perfect driving position.

One complaint we had about the manual car (that the gearlever was too far forward) doesn't really apply to the automatic, especially if you leave the lever in D. Nor were there any complaints about the brake pedal, which is correctly

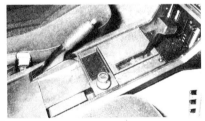

Right: the wedge headed lever controls a Borg Warner 3-speed automatic transmission with ideal ratios. Below: the multi-adjustable steering column and seat provide a near perfect driving position. Below right: the velour-type nylon upholstery is very comfortable and the seats support you in all the right places

Above: the neat door releases and central locking facility are a boon. Below: end-of-instrument-pod fuse mounting is a clever touch

Above: major instruments are a model of clarity but minor switches are fumbly to use, especially in the dark. Below: the commendably capacious boot held 12.7 cu ft of cases

MOTOR ROAD TEST NO 5/77 ●
ROVER 3500 auto

PERFORMANCE

CONDITIONS

Weather	Overcast; wind, 0-10 mph
Temperature	50°-55°F
Barometer	29.8 in Hg
Surface	Damp tarmacadam

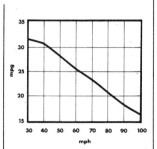

MAXIMUM SPEEDS

	mph	kph
Banked Circuit	120.0	193.1
Best ¼ mile	121.0	194.7
Terminal Speeds:		
at ¼ mile	82	132
at kilometre	101	163
Speed in gears (at 5500 rpm):		
1st	55	88
2nd	90	145

ACCELERATION FROM REST

mph	sec	kph	sec
0-30	3.9	0-40	3.2
0-40	5.4	0-60	5.0
0-50	7.3	0-80	7.2
0-60	9.6	0-100	10.3
0-70	12.4	0-120	13.9
0-80	15.7	0-140	18.8
0-90	20.2	0-160	27.2
0-100	27.6		
Stand'g ¼	17.2	Stand'g km	31.3

ACCELERATION IN KICKDOWN

mph	sec	kph	sec
20-40	3.0	40-60	1.8
30-50	3.4	60-80	2.3
40-60	4.2	80-100	3.0
50-70	5.1	100-120	3.6
60-80	6.1	120-140	4.9
70-90	7.8	140-160	8.4
80-100	11.9		

FUEL CONSUMPTION

Touring	21.1 mpg
	13.4 litres/100 km
Overall	20.6 mpg
	13.7 litres/100 km
Fuel grade	97 octane
	4 star rating

Tank capacity	14.5 galls	
	69.5 litres	
Max range	305 miles	
	490 km	
Test distance	4259 miles	
	6853 km	

*Consumption midway between 30 mph and maximum less 5 per cent for acceleration

SPEEDOMETER (mph)

Speedo							
30	40	50	60	70	80	90	100
True mph							
31	40	49	59	69	78.5	89	99

Distance recorder: 1 per cent fast

WEIGHT

	cwt	kg
Unladen weight*	25.5	1295.5
Weight as tested	29.2	1483.4

*with fuel for approx 50 miles

Performance tests carried out by Motor's staff at the Motor Industry Research Association proving ground, Lindley.

Test Data: World Copyright reserved; no unauthorised reproduction in whole or part.

GENERAL SPECIFICATION

ENGINE

Cylinders	V8
Capacity	3528 cc (215 cu in)
Bore/stroke	88.9×71.1 mm (3.50×2.80 in)
Cooling	Water
Block	Light alloy
Head	Light alloy
Valves	Pushrod ohv
Valve timing	
inlet opens	30° btdc
inlet closes	75° abdc
ex opens	68° bbdc
ex closes	37° atdc
Compression	9.35:1
Carburetter	Twin SU HIF 6
Bearings	5 main
Fuel pump	Submerged electric
Max power	155 bhp (DIN) at 5250 rpm
Max torque	198 lb ft (DIN) at 2500 rpm

TRANSMISSION

Type	3 speed automatic plus torque convertor
Internal ratios and mph/1000 rpm	
Top	1.00:1/23.8
2nd	1.45:1/16.4
1st	2.39:1/9.9
Rev	2.09:1
Final drive	3.08:1

BODY/CHASSIS

Construction	Unitary all steel
Protection	Electrophoretic primer, full undersealant, ventilated sills, zinc-coated outer sill panels, aluminised exhaust system

SUSPENSION

Front	MacPherson struts, coil springs, anti-roll bar
Rear	Live axle located by torque tube, Watts linkage, radius arms, coil springs, Nivomat self-levelling damper struts

STEERING

Type	Rack and pinion
Assistance	Yes
Toe in	0–3 mm
Camber	0°
Castor	2°
King pin	11° 10'

BRAKES

Type	Disc front, drum rear
Servo	Yes
Circuit	Dual
Rear valve	Yes
Adjustment	Self-adjusting

WHEELS

Type	Pressed steel 14×6J
Tyres	Pirelli; 185 HR 14
Pressures	26 psi F/R

ELECTRICAL

Battery	12V, 68Ah
Polarity	Negative
Generator	Alternator 55A
Fuses	11
Headlights	Halogen 60/55W

Make: Rover
Model: 3500 automatic
Maker: Leyland Cars Ltd, Solihull, Warks
Price: £4521.96 basic plus £376.83 car tax plus £391.90 VAT equals £5290.69

---

placed for either right foot or left foot operation. Living with the Rover showed that some of the minor controls and instruments are rather less pleasant than at first appeared. The block of four switches on the right of the instrument binnacle (the front and rear foglamp switches, the hazard warning and the rear demister switches) are fumbly to use, notably in the dark (although the wiper and light stalks on the column are admirable), the fuel gauge is irritatingly hidden, and the speedometer needle hides the first two digits of the tripmeter when the car is stationary — the one time when you most need to read them: refuelling usually takes place while the car is stopped. On the other hand the major dials are clearly calibrated, free of reflections and beautifully lit.

The heating system once again proved excellent, providing plenty of controllable heat, quickly, and to the right areas. However, some heat soak appeared in the ventilation system, for in traffic it would gradually start to emit warmed air. Like our long term test car (but unlike other 3500s we have tried) the vent directly in front of the driver did not seem to be operating properly either, with a very poor flow.

Road noise suppression is generally excellent — one driver believed it came close to Jaguar levels — but there was a distinct thump from the back axle to accompany the jolting already mentioned on cracks in the road. The engine, too, is subdued most of the time, only becoming obtrusive if used to the full.

However, wind noise is excessive. Our long term car suffered from poor door seals, and so did the automatic — it was possible to see daylight around the nearside rear door, past the seal! This created a loud and unpleasant roar at speed over 70 mph which tended to detract from the pleasures of high speed cruising.

Like the previous car the finish of the automatic was generally good, but with irritating faults that seemed therefore all the more prominent. The poor fit of the door seals has been mentioned: on top of that there was an annoying steering vibration period between about 85 and 95 mph (which however may have been due to poor wheel balancing rather than any basic flaw). It was nice to see that at least one running modification has taken place — the single, cheap-looking strap which lifted the tonneau cover when the rear door was opened has been replaced by two rather less objectionable straps, one at each side.

To sum up, we believe the Rover 3500 is a splendid car. Replacing the excellent five-speed gearbox with an automatic has in no way spoilt its character, for it is still a very good high-speed cruiser that is more economical than most of the competition.

The Rivals

Other possible rivals not tested in automatic form include the Renault 30, the BMW 528 and the Citroen CX 2400

ROVER 3500 AUTOMATIC £5291

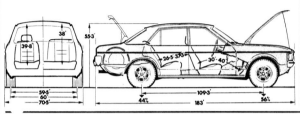

An excellent car which the three-speed automatic transmission enhances. Performance is very nearly as good as that of the manual version, and it is still exceptionally economical for its size and performance. Along with the Renault 30 the most versatile due to hatchback and folding rear seat. Steering and handling excellent in spite of live rear axle. Ride at times is harsh, brakes unprogressive, and door sealing poor

Power, bhp/rpm	155/5250
Torque, lb ft/rpm	198/2500
Tyres	185 HR 14
Weight, cwt	25.5
Max speed, mph	120.0
0-60 mph, sec	9.6
30-50 mph in k'down (sec)	3.4
Overall mpg	20.6
Touring mpg	21.1
Fuel grade (stars)	4
Boot capacity (cu ft)	12.7
Test Date	Jan 22, 1977

FORD GRANADA GHIA £4948

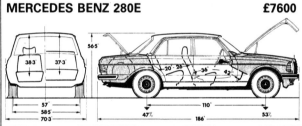

Flagship of Ford's European range. In essence, luxury version of successful and respected Granada with 3-litre engine, automatic transmission and many other features as standard: radio; tinted glass; digital clock; sliding roof; halogen head- and spotlights, for example. Leather cappings and special trim adorn the luxurious interior. Very refined and lots of interior/boot space. An excellent car.

Power, bhp/rpm	138/5000
Torque, lb ft/rpm	176/3000
Tyres	185 SR 14
Weight, cwt	27.1
Max speed, mph	110.2
0-60 mph, sec	10.5
30-50 mph in k'down (sec)	3.7
Overall mpg	17.4
Touring mpg	20.8
Fuel grade (stars)	4
Boot capacity (cu ft)	13.0
Test Date	May 11, 1974

MERCEDES BENZ 280E £7600

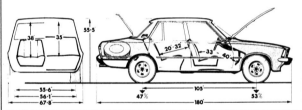

Top model of Mercedes' new W123 small-car range. Only imported to UK in four-speed automatic form. Average performance from smooth dohc engine, though car feels a bit sluggish. Precise, forgiving handling; excellent roadholding. Good accommodation for people and luggage, superb instruments, typically efficient heating and ventilation. An excellent — but expensive — car.

Power, bhp/rpm	177/6000
Torque, lb ft/rpm	172/4500
Tyres	195/70 HR 14
Weight, cwt	28.7
Max speed, mph	117.0
0-60 mph, sec	10.4
30-50 mph in k'down (sec)	5.1
Overall mpg	19.0
Touring mpg	21.0
Fuel grade (stars)	5
Boot capacity (cu ft)	11.2
Test Date	Oct 9, 1976

OPEL COMMODORE GS/E £6421

This Opel is one of the most responsive and best handling of middle-weight saloons. Fuel injected engine gives good performance but with mediocre fuel consumption. Although not very quiet at low speeds, outstandingly refined and fuss-free at speed. GM's auto transmission fitted to test car responsive and smooth. Saloon variant has good accommodation and large boot. Comfortable despite hard seats.

Power, bhp/rpm	160/5400
Torque, lb ft/rpm	168/4200
Tyres	195/70 HR 14
Weight, cwt	24.8
Max speed, mph	116.0
0-60 mph, sec	10.3
30-50 mph in k'down (sec)	3.8
Overall mpg	17.3
Touring mpg	—*
Fuel grade (stars)	4
Boot capacity (cu ft)	12.6
Test Date	Dec 14, 1974

TOYOTA CROWN 2600 £5442

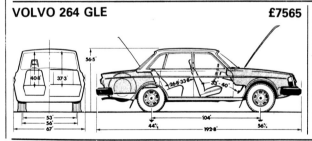

Top Toyota in UK range, and a typical example of a large Japanese car where comfort takes precedence over performance. Plush interior and lavish equipment are very strong selling points. Not especially roomy inside compared with European rivals (Granada, Peugeot 604), nor particularly fast or economical. Quiet except when extended, handling safe but uninspiring. Jerky automatic transmission.

Power, bhp/rpm	150/5400
Torque, lb ft/rpm	164/3800
Tyres	185 SR 14
Weight, cwt	28.5
Max speed, mph	97.3
0-60 mph, sec	13.5
30-50 mph in k'down (sec)	4.4
Overall mpg	16.1
Touring mpg	18.9
Fuel grade (stars)	3
Boot capacity (cu ft)	12.2
Test Date	Dec 13, 1975

VOLVO 264 GLE £7565

Typical model from this Swedish company—well finished, safe, reliable, but rather dull. Performance and fuel consumption of test car were below average and disappointing, but perhaps car was not representative. Like Renault 30 and Peugeot 604 has PRV engine, but with fuel injection to produce 145 bhp. Standard equipment includes heated seat and "daylight running lights" as well as electronic ignition. Figures, right, are from the now superseded GL model.

Power, bhp/rpm	145/6000
Torque, lb ft/rpm	150/3000
Tyres	185/70 HR 14
Weight, cwt	27.3
Max speed, mph	103.7
0-60 mph, sec	12.5
30-50 mph in k'down (sec)	4.8
Overall mpg	15.9
Touring mpg	—*
Fuel grade (stars)	3
Boot capacity (cu ft)	13.1
Test Date	June 14, 1976

*fuel injected

AutoTEST

Rover 2300

Last to appear in the SD1 series, the 2300 has a quiet ride, admirable steering, handling and roadholding, together with practical and excellent internal carrying capacity. The smallest Rover straight six gives smooth but unremarkable performance and disappointing economy. Poor value for money in relation to the 2600 version.

Above: At the limit of adhesion the Rover understeers considerably, and also rolls noticeably. The stainless steel front bumper has moulded plastic "add on" corners
Below: Except for the badge the 2300 rear is identical to the 2600. The back bumper is also stainless steel, with moulded plastic corners. A heated rear window is standard

TWO YEARS AGO the "ultimate" Rover did not exist as far as the public was concerned. Since then the inevitable expansion of the model range has led to the introduction of the 2300/2600 series last October. Production delays and cash flow considerations have meant that the cheapest, though by no means cheap, 2300 has taken until now to filter through. Perhaps because it was intended as a replacement for the old 2200 it would be fair to say that the 2300 is further from the 2600 in specification than the 2600 is from the 3500.

Although our test car was fitted with the optional five-speed gearbox, and power steering, prospective owners can take note of the fourth gear figures as it is their top gear ratio on the basic model. Fifth is simply an overdrive giving just under 25 mph per 1,000 rpm, while all the lower ratios are the same as in the five-speed gearbox. Nor does the overall gearing differ from the 2600, both cars having the same 3.45 to 1 final drive and 175/14 HR tyres. The 2300 specification does not include

the self-levelling rear suspension that is standard on the "up market" cars, and in its place variable rate coil springs suffice. Also lacking is the full instrument panel of the 2600/3500 and slightly simpler cloth trim is fitted, together with different wheel trims and, of course, badges.

The smaller capacity has been achieved with the minimum of engineering. An 8mm reduction in stroke from 84mm to 76mm does the job. The 2300 power unit measures 81mm by 76mm, and apart from the shorter throw crankshaft, Rover have managed to get away with only an alternative piston with different crown-to-gugeon-pin height, that because of its shallower dish and smaller valve cut-outs gives the same compression ratio of 9.25 to 1 and makes up for the shorter stroke without shortening the cylinder block or lengthening the con rods. In every other respect the four main bearing 2,350 c.c. straight six is similar to the 2600 unit and gives 123 bhp at 5,000 rpm and 134 lb ft torque at 4,000 rpm against figures for the 2600 of 136 bhp at 5,000 rpm and 152 lb ft at 3,750 rpm.

Interestingly our kerb weight for the 2300 was exactly the same as for our Autotest 2600 (22 September 1977) at 26.4 cwt, and it might be worth reminding the reader that the Rover SD1 shape has one of the lower drag co-efficients in the family car business at 0.39.

Performance and economy

There is an unwritten law determining that beyond a certain point the fitting of a smaller engine has little effect on economy, and an adverse effect on performance. Naturally the 2300 is somewhat slower overall than the 2600, but more so in the mid-range, where it might be better to compare the performance figures with the average 2-litre family car. High gearing plays a part here. The close-on 90 mph third gear will take the Rover from 50-70 mph in 8.4 sec, while the same exercise in fourth requires 12.5 sec. Compare this with a 2-litre Cortina in top gear as it is unlikely that the driver would change down, and we have a time of ³ sec. However a measure of the ι. drag co-efficient that the 2300 body shape offers must lie in a mean maximum speed of 111 mph achieved in direct fourth gear, and corresponding to 5,350 rpm. 350 rpm beyond the peak of the power curve. The identically geared 2600 managed to pull its 117 mph top speed and 4,680 rpm in overdrive fifth, whereas it ran out of breath in fourth gear, only reaching 113 mph and 5,430 rpm. Popping the 2300 into overdrive fifth around the banked circuit at MIRA, the speed slowly decayed to a mean average of 107 mph (4,300 rpm).

Both the maximum speed and a 0-60 mph time of 11.9 sec just failed to match up to works performance claims, conceivably due to the fact that our test car had covered a mere 1,000 miles on taking the figures and might still have been a little tight. Notwithstanding we were able to ʰ ᵉr the claimed 0-30 mph time by ι ᵴec at 3.9 sec. The high first gear made any wheelspin impossible to generate, and it might be of interest to those considering towing a caravan, that we could not restart on the 1 in 3 test hill, whereas the similarly geared but much more torquey 2600 managed this without any problem.

The engine has all the characteristics of, and indeed has, very conservative valve timing. As we have said actual performance is nothing outstanding in the mid-range, as times of 5.0 sec for 30-50 mph in second gear, and 7.5 sec for 40-60 mph in third show. However this is to some extent made up for by excellent flexibility. The straight six would accept full throttle, and pull without hesitation from 10 mph in fourth gear (500 rpm). Some idea of the flat power curve can be gained from the consistency of the figures throughout the 20 mph increments in any particular gear. For instance 10-30 mph in top took 11.7 sec, while a more normally used 40-60 mph in the same gear still required 11.4 sec. Totally lacking any "cammyness",

Above: The detachable rear shelf lifts with the rear door and covers the "normal" luggage compartment. Only its removal and folding the rear seat are required to convert into an estate Below: The 2300 wheel trims are plain grey plastic, and help to identify the smaller-engined car

the engine could be made, when pressed hard, to sing smoothly in the gears way past peak power at 5,000 rpm. Using 6,000 rpm in the well spaced ratios for the acceleration runs we saw maxima in first, second, and third, of 37, 59, and 89 mph, and it is this high intermediate and overall gearing that gives the 2300 its ability to cruise smoothly and quietly. However, one wonders if perhaps a slightly lower rear axle ratio

might not be justified when the car is fitted with the five-speed transmission.

An overall fuel consumption of 22.0 mpg compared with 22.4 mpg for the Autotest 2600 can be regarded as identical, and seems to bear out the comments made in our first paragraph. The implication is that the smaller engine is working harder to maintain the higher cruising speeds. Above 70 mph 2300 constant speed fuel consumption figures are marginally worse than its bigger brother, but still within a reasonable three per cent that could easily be accounted for by different conditions or experimental error. Nevertheless 27.8 mpg at a constant 70 mph in fifth, and 17.4 mpg at 100 mph are notable figures for a big car. If you bear in mind that they fall to over 31 mpg at 60 mph, down to 43.8 mpg at 30 mph, where our 2600 was only doing 34 mpg, it is less than obvious why the overall figure is a little disappointing. Road driving conditions do tend to give the lie to experimental measurement, and possibly because of the smaller engine's lack of low-down "bite", more throttle than usual is required to keep up with the traffic flow. It is also unlikely that one

would drive for long distances in fifth gear at speeds where economy gains are significant. As a matter of interest we have also printed the fourth gear fuel figures for potential purchasers of a four-speed 2300.

Handling, roadholding steering and brakes

We have praised the 2600 and 3500 in this department before, and without change in kerb weight or its distribution praise is again due. With 55 per cent of the vehicle weight over the front wheels understeer naturally predominates, but it is something that will only be encountered at abnormally high cornering speeds. Lifting off produces the normal tuck-in effect — or more neutral characteristic, as the car slows and the front tyres regain their grip. To their credit Rover have used a torque tube rear axle with its degree of natural anti-squat on all the 2300/2600/3500 series. Further located by two trailing arms and a Watts linkage the system has enabled anti-dive to be dispensed with on the MacPerson strut front end as braking torque tends to make the rear sit down. Even without the self-levelling rear suspension of the

The straight six leaves plenty of room under the bonnet to get at items requiring maintenance. The large trunking leads to the air inlet temperature control valve (hidden behind the strut mounting on the nearside). The battery, water expansion header tank, and brake and clutch fluid reservoirs are mounted on the offside

2600/3500 and only variable rate springs, the rear dips very little under acceleration, and yet puts down the admittedly smaller amount of power very well, especially in the wet. Some axle hop can be provoked when accelerating hard over ruts and potholes, but otherwise the rear wheels stay defiantly glued to the road.

Directional stability is less impressive. Mild crosswinds on a motorway gave the car a nervous wander that aroused comment from all who drove the 2300 and yet, as everybody agreed, basic stability was very good. One soon learnt to ignore the phenomenon, as constant steering correction tended to make matters worse.

Having provided the range with power steering, it is nice to experience a sane degree of assistance, and slightly higher gearing than average with "only" 2¾ turns from lock to lock. Definitely "European" in feel, it is direct, sensitive, and to quote our 2600 test "avoids the go karting over-response that is a feature of the Citroën SM or CX." As it is the 2300 can be manoeuvred around town without changing your grip on the steering wheel, and accurately flicked through sweeping country bends with confidence using very small wheel movements. A member of the staff who has driven a 2300 without power steering felt that it was the first choice on the option list, bearing in mind the 4½ relatively

heavy turns of the standard system.

The brakes are on the light side but thankfully do not suffer from being over-sensitive. Required pedal pressures range downwards from the 70 lb needed for our best 0.98G stop with the rear brakes just locking, to the first increment in the response test at 20 lb and 0.35G. With only the driver on board the rear brakes locked rather too early in the wet, suggesting that the brake balance has been altered from the 2600, whose front brakes tended to lock early. Sharing the same brakes as the 2600, the 2300 absorbed the standard 10 0.5G fade searching stops from 75 mph without protest by way of smell or fade; though there was some shudder from the front discs during the last three stops.

The handbrake proved entirely satisfactory, holding the car easily in both directions on a 1 in 3 slope, also managing an acceptable 0.3G retardation from 30 mph on dry flat tarmac.

Behind the wheel

To the driver, the Rover 2300 immediately feels right. The steering column is adjustable for both rake and reach from a firm but supportive driving seat. A very tall driver might prefer a little more rearward adjustment for his seat but overall it is one of the best ergonomic packages that we have come across in a family car, and typified by a driving seat that rises slightly as it is pulled forward

keeping over-the-bonnet vision constant for the shorter driver. The five speed gearchange has the now almost universal H pattern with a dog leg change into fifth. Conceivably because the test car had covered such a low mileage, the movement felt rather notchy particularly on the downchange into second gear. Driving the 2300 there is something of a thoroughbred feel — quiet but also responsive without any rubbery compliance that has become common in the search for silent motoring. Not so good is the threequarter rear visibility, and one soon acquires the habit of making good use of the effective internally adjustable door mirrors. Surprisingly there is no provision for a rear window wiper.

As we said in the introduction, cost saving has required that the 2300 has a far more basic and shorter instrument panel, lacking a revcounter and oil pressure gauge. The minor controls are common to all models with the right hand column stalk for the indicators, horn, dip/main beam, and headlamp flash, while the two-speed plus manual intermittent wipers and windscreen wash are triggered from the left stalk. Attached to the column nacelle is the small side and headlight switch which sensibly cannot be confused with any other control. The test car was fitted with the optional halogen headlights which gave plenty of power and spread on both full and dipped beam.

The 2300 instrument panel lacks a rev counter and is therefore shorter than the 2600 example. The speedometer is flanked on the right by a fresh air outlet, fuel, battery, and water temperature gauges. The right-hand column stalk controls the indicators, headlamp dipping and flashing, and also the horn, while the left-hand stalk looks after the windscreen wash/wipe and intermittent wipe. The steering column itself is adjustable for both rake and reach. The heating and ventilation controls are in the centre console above which are the radio and two ventilation outlets. Note the convoluted hot air duct leading to the door. The main light switch is tucked away on the steering column shroud. The hazard warning, heated rear window and fog light switches are to the left of the water temperature gauge. The centre console houses the choke lever and cigarette lighter

Specification

ENGINE	
Cylinders	Front, rear drive
Cylinders	6
Main bearings	4
Cooling	Water
Fan	Viscous
Bore, mm (in.)	81mm (3.2)
Stroke, mm (in.)	76mm (3.0)
Capacity, cc (in³)	2,350 cc (92.5)
Valve gear	ohc
Camshaft drive	Chain
Compression ratio	9.25-to-1
Octane rating	97 RM
Carburettors	2 SU HS6
Max power	123 bhp (DIN) at 5,000 rpm
Max torque	134 lb ft at 4,000 rpm

TRANSMISSION
Type: Five-speed all-syncromesh manual

Gear	Ratio	mph/1000rpm
Top	0.83 to 1	24.9
4th	1.00 to 1	20.7
3rd	1.40 to 1	14.9
2nd	2.09 to 1	9.9
1st	3.32 to 1	6.2
Final drive gear	Hypoid bevel	
Ratio	3.45 to 1	

SUSPENSION
Front—location	MacPherson struts, lower links
springs	Coil
dampers	Telescopic
anti-roll bar	Yes
Rear—location	Live axle, torque tube, watts linkage
springs	Coil
dampers	Telescopic
anti-roll bar	No

STEERING
Type	Rack and pinion
Power assistance	Optional (fitted to test car)
Wheel diameter	15.5 in

BRAKES
Front	10.1 in. dia. disc
Rear	9.0 in. dia. drum
Servo	Yes

WHEELS
Type	Pressed steel disc
Rim width	5½ in J section
Tyres—make	Various — Goodyear G800 Grandprix on test car
—type	Radial
—size	175HR 14

EQUIPMENT
Battery	12 volt 50 Ah
Alternator	55 amp
Headlamps	4 lamp hologen 120/220 Watt total
Reversing lamp	Standard
Hazard warning	Standard
Electric fuses	10
Screen wipers	2-speed + manual intermit.
Screen washer	Electric
Interior heater	Air blending
Interior trim	Cloth seats, cloth headlining
Floor covering	Carpet
Jack	Screw pillar type
Jacking points	4/2 at front/ 2 at rear
Windscreen	Laminated
Underbody protection	Bitumastic and plastisol sill cover

MAINTENANCE
Fuel tank	14.5 Imp. galls (65.9 litres)
Cooling system	18.2 pints (inc. heater)
Engine sump	11.2 pints SAE 20/50
Gearbox	2.8 pints SAE 80EP
Final drive	1.6 pints
Grease	No points
Valve clearance	Inlet 0.018 in. (cold) Exhaust 0.018 in. (cold)
Contact breaker	0.015 in. gap
Ignition timing	10 deg BTDC (static)
Spark plug —type	Champion BN9Y 14mm taper seat
—gap	0.024-0.026 in.
Tyre pressures	F28; R30 psi (normal driving)
Max payload	1,180 lb (536 kg)

Maximum Speeds

Gear	mph	kph	rpm
Top (mean)	107	172	4,300
(best)	109	175	4,375
4th	111	179	5,350
3rd	89	143	6,000
2nd	59	95	6,000
1st	37	60	6,000

Acceleration

True mph	Time (sec)	Speedo mph
30	3.9	29
40	6.1	40
50	8.7	50
60	11.9	60
70	16.4	71
80	21.4	81
90	29.9	92
100	41.8	102
110	—	
120	—	

Standing ¼-mile:
18.7 sec, 75 mph
kilometre:
34.3 sec, 93 mph

mph	Top	4th	3rd	2nd
10-30	—	11.7	8.7	5.3
20-40	16.1	11.6	7.8	5.1
30-50	15.0	11.2	7.6	5.0
40-60	15.9	11.4	7.5	5.8
50-70	18.2	12.5	8.4	—
60-80	21.9	14.2	10.0	—
70-90	28.5	16.9	13.8	—

Consumption

Fuel
Overall mpg: 22.0
(12.9 litres/100km)
Calculated (DIN) mpg: 25.3
(11.2 litres/100km)

Constant speed:

mph	mpg 5th gear	4th gear
30	43.8	38.2
40	42.5	37.2
50	37.4	33.9
60	31.4	29.3
70	27.8	24.9
80	24.4	20.3
90	20.5	17.7
100	17.4	15.7

Brakes

Fade (from 75 mph in neutral)
Pedal load for 0.5g stops in lb

	start/end		start/end
1	30/25	6	30/50
2	30/30	7	30/45
3	30/30	8	30/45
4	30/30	9	30/50
5	30/40	10	40/50

Response (from 30 mph in neutral)

Load	g	Distance
20lb	0.35	86ft
30	0.55	55
40	0.70	43
50	0.82	37
60	0.91	33
70	0.98	31
Handbrake	0.3	100
Max. gradient 1 in 3		

Clutch
Pedal 55lb and 6.6 in.

Autocar formula
Hard driving, difficult conditions
20.0 mpg
Average driving, average conditions
24.0 mpg
Gentle driving, easy conditions
28.0 mpg
Grade of fuel: Premium, 4-star
(97 RM)
Mileage recorder: 2 per cent overreading

Official fuel consumption figures
(ECE laboratory test conditions; not necessarily related to Autocar figures):
Urban cycle — 17.5 mpg
Steady 56 mph — 36.8 mpg
Steady 75 mph — 31.0 mpg

Oil
Consumption (SAE 20/50)
700 miles/pint

Test Conditions

Wind 12-18 mph
Temperature 8 deg C (45 deg F)
Barometer 29.5 in. Hg
Humidity 70 per cent
Surface dry asphalt and concrete
Test distance 1,392 miles

Figures taken at 1,238 miles by our own staff at the Motor Industry Research Association proving ground at Nuneaton.

All Autocar test results are subject to world copyright and may not be reproduced in whole or part without the Editor's written permission

Regular Service

Interval

Change	3,000	6,000	12,000
Engine oil	Check	Yes	Yes
Oil filter	No	Yes	Yes
Gearbox oil	No	Yes	Yes
Spark plugs	No	No	Yes
Air cleaner	No	No	Yes
C/breaker	No	No	Yes

| **Total cost** | **£9.75** | **£36.75** | **£40.00** |

(Assuming labour at £6.50/hour)

Parts Cost

(including VAT)

Brake pads (2 wheels) —front	£13.33
Brake shoes (2 wheels) —rear	£18.46
Complete exhaust system	£63.72
Tyre — each (typical advertised)	£37.35
Windscreen	£73.20
Headlamp unit	£26.26
Front wing	£47.52
Rear bumper	£37.80

Warranty Period
12 months unlimited mileage +supercover

Weight

Kerb
26.4 cwt/2,954 lb/1,341 kg
(Distribution F/R, 55/45)
As tested
29.5 cwt/3,308 lb/1,502 kg

Boot capacity: 14.4/22.4 cu ft.

Turning circles:
Between kerbs
L, 33ft 11in.; R, 34ft 2in.
Between walls
L, 36ft 3in.; R, 36ft 6in.
Turns, lock to lock 2.7

Test Scorecard

(Average of scoring by Autocar Road Test team)

Ratings:
6 Excellent
5 Good
4 Above average
3 Below average
2 Poor
1 Bad

PERFORMANCE	4.3
STEERING AND HANDLING	4.6
BRAKES	4.2
COMFORT IN FRONT	4.8
COMFORT IN BACK	4.0
DRIVERS AIDS	4.1
(instruments, lights, wipers, visibility etc.)	
CONTROLS	4.2
NOISE	4.7
STOWAGE	4.7
ROUTINE SERVICE	4.3
(under-bonnet access, dipstick etc.)	
EASE OF DRIVING	4.1

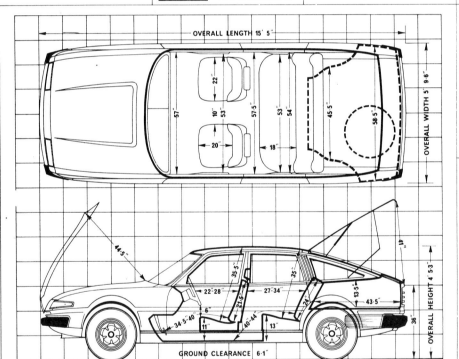

OVERALL LENGTH 15' 5"
OVERALL WIDTH 5' 9.6"
OVERALL HEIGHT 4' 5.3"
GROUND CLEARANCE 6.1"
WHEELBASE 9' 2.8"
FRONT TRACK 4' 11.1"
REAR TRACK 4' 11.1"

Comparisons

	Price (£)	Max mph	0-60 (sec)	Overall mpg	Capacity (c.c.)	Power (bhp)	Wheelbase (in.)	Length (in.)	Width (in.)	Kerb wt. (lb)	Fuel (gal)	Tyre size
Rover 2300	5,645	111	11.9	22.0	2,350	123	110.5	185.0	69.0	2,954	14.5	175-14
Citroën CX 2400	5,428	113	11.8	23.5	2,347	115	112.0	181.0	68.0	2,990	15.0	175-14
Renault 30TS	6,125	117	9.8	18.5	2,664	125	105.0	178.0	68.0	2,844	14.0	175-14
Volvo 244 GL	6,231	106	11.4	21.3	2,127	123	104.0	182.0	67.0	2,950	13.2	185/70-14
*Ford Granada 2.3 GL	5,519	98	14.5	20.6	2,293	108	109.0	187.5	70.5	2,915	14.2	175-14
Audi Avant 1600	5,099	100	12.6	26.9	1,558	85	105.5	180.5	70.0	2,440	13.2	165-14
Peugeot 604 SL	6,611	113	9.4	19.6	2,664	136	110.3	186.0	69.8		15.5	175-14
Lancia Gamma Berlina	7,136	—	—	—	2,484	140	105.0	180.0	68.0	—	13.9	185/70-14

*Performance figures for Automatic

Comfort and convenience

There is an air of sensible practicality about the interior. The vinyl covered facia and instrument panel could be criticised for looking a little "hand finished" in the odd corner, but generally the occupants ride in restful quality surroundings. The rear seats are individually shaped, but not to the extent that would preclude carrying a third passenger, having folded up the rather clever centre armrest. Surprisingly the rear seat passengers do not have overmuch head and leg room, though such comments only apply to people over six feet tall, and with the front seats pushed back as far as possible. Two large gloveboxes, a deep and wide facia shelf, and lipped rear parcel tray (removed in the conversion into an estate) should give enough storage space for any sensible amount of travelling paraphernalia.

The powerful air blending heating and ventilation is well able to cater for all tastes and conditions. Positioned vertically on the centre console are four levers to control hot and cold air direction and quantity, heat, and fan boost. Their operation is precise and straightforward, except at night when lack of any illumination prompts a moment's thought. Fan boost, which is necessary for any noticeable degree of ventilation, is thankfully almost inaudible on the slowest of three speeds. Demisting air is ducted to both the screen and front door windows to keep them clear of condensation.

The 2300 ride is solid, rather than over-soft, and "comfortable." A reassuring lack of roll, and perhaps helped by its length, little pitch further conveys a taut feel to the car. At the same time the long travel suspension is well able to soak up large undulations, keeping the car commendably level. Road noise is thoroughly controlled, though some thump and rumble is understandably transmitted through to the interior when running over poor surfaces. Those who have driven all three engine variants have commented that the 2300 has by comparison with the long stroke 2600 a far smoother feel, which made motorway cruising a pleasure. Were it not for speed limits, putting 100 miles into the hour would neither be a strain on the ears or the car, and as it is the 2300 simply whispers along at the legal limit.

Living with the Rover 2300

The sheer practicality of the Rover 2300 takes some beating when it comes to carrying any loads. Its conversion into an estate takes but a minute, and provides over 22 cubic feet of space, slightly more than in a Renault 20/30 series. For normal touring there is still a 14 cubic feet boot behind the rear seat, and if pressed, small articles can be placed underneath the boot floor next to the spare wheel, which is deleted if the car is equipped with the optional Denovo tyres. Loading through the easy to open rear door is easy enough, though the rear sill is quite high, which might present problems

Above: The rear seat features a centre armrest, which when folded away gives enough room for three people in the back. Note the lipped tray behind the seat

Above right: With the front seats adjusted fully back there is adequate space for a six-foot person to sit, though leg room is a little restricted

Above: With the rear shelf removed, and the back seat folded down, the Rover has an extremely generous carrying capacity

Left: The "normal" boot holds just over 14 cu ft of luggage. The hinged shelf is attached to the rear door by two very quickly detachable straps

Below left: "Halfway house" with the rear seat in place but no rear parcel shelf. Gas struts hold the rear door open

Below: The spare wheel is hidden under the boot floor with the jack

of trying to lift over something very heavy.

The 14.5 gallon fuel tank should give a comfortable range of 300 miles between fuel stops, while day to day maintenance of underbonnet items is simple and straightforward. There are 10 fuses beneath a cover at the end of the instrument panel.

In conclusion

The Rover 2300 completes the SD1 series and has enough qualities to justify its manufacture. However, disregarding the less important options fitted to our test car but including power steering and five-speed transmission, its price is still over £6,000 and within £200 of a similarly equipped 2600, which has much better instrumentation and self levelling rear suspension. Bearing this in mind, and the lack of any practical economy gains from the smaller engine, the 2600 would seem a far better buy, and is bound to be more sought after on the second-hand market. Although the 2300 has nothing remarkable in the way of mid-range performance (prospective towing owners please note) it does offer exceptionally quiet cruising, and the expected excellent SD1 steering, handling, and ride qualities. ☐

MANUFACTURER:
Rover-Triumph
British Leyland Ltd.
P.O. Box 2
Lode Lane
Solihull, Warks.

PRICES	
Basic	£4,825.00
Special Car Tax	£402.08
VAT	£418.17
Total (in GB)	**£5,645.25**
Seat Belts	incl
Licence	£50.00
Delivery charge (London)	£40.00
Number plates	£10.00
Total on the Road	
(exc. insurance)	**£5,745.25**
Insurance	Group 6
Extras (inc. VAT)	
Automatic transmission	£330.21
*Five-speed gearbox	£159.49
*Power steering	£201.86
Denovo wheels and tyres	£94.99
Tinted glass	£74.77
*Halogen headlights	£34.27
*Metallic paint	£47.97
Leather seat facings	£198.90
*Remote control passenger	
door mirror	£27.05
*Fitted to test car	
TOTAL AS TESTED	
ON THE ROAD	**£6,215.89**

My faithful Rover

No major disasters, only a few minor trim and equipment failings, have struck Philip Turner's Rover 2600. At home and abroad it has shown the performance and enjoyable handling of a good sporting saloon

THEY SAID it when the P4 with its cyclops eye appeared in September, 1950. They said it again when the SD1 was unveiled in July, 1976. "It's not a Rover," they said. Yet each in succession — so far — has proved to be the most successful model Rover had built. I knew from the start that the 3500 V-8 engined Rover would in due course have a six cylinder brother which I managed to persuade my Editor would be just the car for *Motor*'s man in the Midlands, so we ordered one, and then we waited and we waited as various crises kept putting back the release date. But finally, in October, 1977 the 2600 was announced, with its new single overhead camshaft engine developed and built by the Triumph end of Rover-Triumph at Canley where it had begun life as an intended replacement for the six cylinder Triumph engine. Much discussed at one time, in fact, was the proposal that the 2600 version of the SD1 should be called a Triumph and not a Rover. Although one can state an excellent case for calling it either, the six cylinder car is indeed quite different in character from the V-8, being much more sporting in feel and therefore much more of a Triumph than a Rover. And if they'd called it a Triumph, I doubt whether people would have made such disparaging comparisons about its much higher noise level than the V-8.

I took delivery of my Rover on April 24, 1978. It had completed 12,000 miles by mid-October and is now well over the 17,000 mark. It has been completely reliable, very comfortable and most enjoyable to drive. Only details of its trim and equipment let it down.

First Impressions
overwhelming first impression was sheer surprise that such a big car should seem to shrink from behind the steering wheel. This impression is, I believe due to a combination of good forward visibility and light, precise steering, for if you can see where you're going and can place the car with confidence, then it becomes very much easier to drive, no matter how big its overall dimensions. On the other hand, for so big a car there seemed surprisingly little room inside the body. The driver's seat did not go back as far as I would have wished, one sat up in the roof, as it were, with the top of the windscreen only just above one's eye level, and getting into and out of the rear compartment called for a certain agility. To such an extent that Mrs Lord Mayor of Birmingham found a 3500 unsuitable as a mayoral chariot for official occasions.

Having lived with a wedge before — I had so early a 2200 off the production line that it was an Austin and not a Princess — I knew that backing into a parking space was fraught with peril owing to the high tail line, but on the other hand the much lower scuttle of the Rover,

thanks to not having a skyscraper-tall long stroke transverse engine to surmount, meant that forward visibility was much better. Even so, a chap from Rolls-Royce told me that when he first took delivery of his Rover, he was for ever leaving apologetic notes on peoples' windscreens in car parks on account of there being more nose below the sight line than he had allowed for.

But my second overwhelming impression was one of relief, that in spite of its smaller engine the 2600 did not feel underpowered and soggy by comparison with the 3500. On the contrary, the acceleration and the general liveliness of the performance made it an exciting car to drive.

The performance I have already mentioned, but the way in which the car comes alive when the tachometer goes sweeping past the 3000 rpm mark and one receives a hard push in the back as it accelerates past the car ahead means overtaking is completed in swift security and is really quite something. And if then one changes up into "top top" it will cruise very happily in fifth gear at well over the indicated 100 mark and still have plenty in hand.

Moreover, the car has the steering, the handling and the brakes to enable this performance to be used with a quiet mind. I thought the power steering a little light when I first came to it, but have now grown thoroughly accustomed to it and

bonnet matters, the clean almost classic lines of the engine. It was, I believe, Sir William Lyons who when that classic Jaguar XK six was being designed, insisted that it should be a good looking engine, so that owners would be proud rather than ashamed to open the bonnet. This is a good looking engine.

Is it a good looking car? Yes, I think it is, a view supported by the head of a Finnish pottery at which we stopped on our travels who said it was one of the best looking cars he'd seen for a very long time. And this in a country which has a world wide reputation for good, clean design. Certainly, it is a car that impresses, so that chaps on the factory gate are apt to find you a special parking

Likes
Everyone who has ridden in the car, even those who have struggled into the rear compartment where, once in situ, they find they have plenty of room to stretch, has remarked on the sheer comfort of the car. It may feel compact to the driver, but to the passengers it gives a big-car ride and that hard to define big-car feeling of stability and comfort. Unlike some cars, however, which are heaven for the passengers but hell for the driver, the Rover is most enjoyable to drive.

never have that horrid feeling of wondering what the front wheels are up to. Perhaps the best tribute I can pay to the steering, brakes and handling is to say that I greatly enjoyed a return run from Wales over roads that twisted their way over the mountains.

As well as liking the general character of the car, there are a number of good small points. Such details as the big screw cap for the oil filler orifice which has a pleasantly solid engineering feel to it, a dipstick that is easy to get at — and to replace and, while dealing with under the

space when all the usual ones are full.

Dislikes
This may shatter people, but I wish the Rover was not a hatchback but had a normal boot. I have in the past had several hatchbacks, a Renault 16, a Reliant Scimitar GTE and liked them so much that until now I would have opted for a hatchback as my first choice. But I think the Rover is too big for a hatchback. Having to heave up that vast rear panel just to toss small items into the luggage

continued over

compartment is altogether too much effort and seems slightly ridiculous. Moreover, the key hole is concealed in all that decorative grille work on the rear panel and is facing downwards towards the road, so to insert the key one has to crouch down in the knees bend position and feel it in. I suppose it depends on one's lifestyle. If every weekend you are loading saddles, camping gear or outboard engines into your car, then certainly the Rover's hatchback feature must be well worth having. But I don't.

I dislike the interior trim which I think looks somewhat poverty-stricken and not worthy of the general high standard of the car. A facia in metal with a black crackle finish can look splendid but the same finish looks cheap when executed in plastic mouldings with synthetic leather trim. The instrument pod, too, looks almost as though added as an afterthought, like a bank of test instruments fitted temporarily to a car in course of development. The four auxiliary instruments have to be peered at round the steering wheel rim, and even when located, the petrol gauge is unreliable when fuel is running low: it then fluctuates wildly. This, I understand is due to the fuel tank being L-shaped, the gauge operating efficiently when recording fuel in the long stroke of the L but becoming confused when dealing with fuel left in the short stroke. Nor do I like the bank of push button switches which you push for "on" and then push again for "off". Is the heated rear window off already and has that last push, in

Above: engine has a big classic look, a well engineered oil filler cap and accessible dip stick

Left: interior has 'big car feel' but rather spartan atmosphere

Right: the small push/push switches are confusing while the auxiliary instruments are masked by the steering wheel

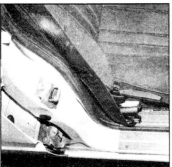
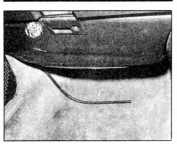

12,000 MILE REPORT ● ROVER 2600*

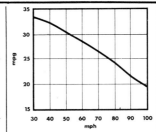
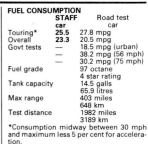

PERFORMANCE

Data for Rover 2600 road test car

CONDITIONS
Weather	Overcast; wind 0-8 mph
Temperature	50-54°F
Barometer	29.8 in Hg
Surface	Dry tarmacadam

MAXIMUM SPEEDS
	mph	kph
Banked Circuit	117.8	189.5
Best ¼ mile	120.8	194.4
Terminal Speeds:		
at ¼ mile	84	135
at kilometre	104	167
at mile	84	134
Speed in gears (at 6400 rpm):		
1st	37	60
2nd	60	97
3rd	89	143

ACCELERATION FROM REST
mph	sec	kph	sec
0-30	3.2	0-40	2.6
0-40	4.8	0-60	4.3
0-50	6.7	0-80	6.7
0-60	9.0	0-100	9.7
0-70	12.4	0-120	14.0
0-80	15.7	0-140	19.0
0-90	20.5	0-160	27.5
0-100	27.5		
0-110	38.8		
Stand'g ¼	17.1	Stand'g km	31.2

ACCELERATION IN TOP
mph	sec	kph	sec
20-40	12.5	40-60	8.0
30-50	11.7	60-80	7.1
40-60	12.2	80-100	7.7
50-70	12.2	100-120	7.7
60-80	13.0	120-140	10.0
70-90	14.6		

ACCELERATION IN 4TH
mph	sec	kph	sec
20-40	9.0	40-60	5.4
30-50	8.4	60-80	5.3
40-60	8.4	80-100	5.3
50-70	8.4	100-120	5.3
60-80	8.8	120-140	7.0
70-90	10.0	140-160	7.2
80-100	12.9		

FUEL CONSUMPTION
	STAFF car	Road test car
Touring*	25.5	27.8 mpg
Overall	23.3	20.5 mpg
Govt tests	—	18.5 mpg (urban)
	—	38.2 mpg (56 mph)
	—	30.2 mpg (75 mph)
Fuel grade		97 octane
		4 star rating
Tank capacity		14.5 galls
		65.9 litres
Max range		403 miles
		648 km
Test distance		1982 miles
		3189 km

*Consumption midway between 30 mph and maximum less 5 per cent for acceleration.

SPEEDOMETER (mph)
Speedo	30	40	50	60	70	80	90	100
True mph	29	38.5	48	57	66	75	85	94

Distance recorder: 1 per cent fast

WEIGHT
	cwt	kg
Unladen weight*	25.6	1300.5
Weight as tested	29.3	1488.5

*with fuel for approx 50 miles

Performance tests carried out by Motor's staff at the Motor Industry Research Association proving ground, Lindley.

Test Data: World Copyright reserved; no unauthorised reproduction in whole or part.

COMPARISONS
	Capacity cc	Price £	Max mph	0-60 sec	30-50 sec	Overall mpg	Touring mpg	Length in	Width in	Weight cwt	Boot cu ft
Rover 2600	**2597**	**6795**	**117.8**	**9.0**	**8.4**	**20.5**	**27.8**	**185.0**	**69.8**	**25.6**	**12.7**
Audi 100 GL 5E	2144	6940	113.1	9.5	9.1	22.0	—*	184.3	69.5	23.1	14.0
Citroen CX GTi	2347	7303	114.5	10.1	7.1	20.1	—*	181.0	68.0	25.8	10.2
Ford Granada 2.8iGLS	2792	7163	117.4	9.0	9.3	20.4	—*	187.0	70.5	26.1	13.2
Renault 30 TS	2664	6490	114.0	9.2	7.8	19.7	23.4	178.0	68.5	24.7	11.8
Volvo 244 GLE	2127	7036	108.0	10.5	10.1	24.0	—*	192.8	67.0	26.2	13.1

*Fuel injected, so not measured

Top: boot key hole is hard to locate. Centre: seat belts often fail to retract fully. Above: trim under glove box keeps coming adrift

fact, switched it on? Difficult to tell, for the blue light in the bank of signal lights which lights up when the window heating is on pales into invisibility on a sunny day. I much prefer switches which you click down for on and up for off, for not only are *hey more easy to locate by feel — at st I was for ever prodding the wrong push button and switching on the fog warning lights — but also one can tell at a touch whether they are on or off.

The best switches of this type I have so far come across were the bank of finger tip switches on the Austin/Princess 2200. In short, I would like to see a redesign job done on the instrumentation and general layout of the whole of the facia.

Any other dislikes? Well, I know there is too much engine noise for a car of this type, but possibly owing to the fact I have spent so many years around racing pits and paddocks, I am less sensitive to noise than most people. I even find the throaty snarl the engine gives vent to above 4000 rpm a stirring and exciting sound.

Reliability

Only minor failings of trim and equipment have prevented the Rover from being a totally fault free car. Engine, transmission and suspension have never failed in any respect. The engine ran somewhat lumpily on tick over and owing to the fact that it sits on fairly hard mountings due to shortage of room under the bonnet, this makes itself felt inside the car, but this was attended to at an early service. As was a rattle underneath caused by the handbrake cable. The trim on both sides of the boot had to be stuck back into place, also the trim under the locker on the passenger's side of the facia which has since come adrift again. Then first the driver's seat belt refused to retract and then the passenger's seat belt followed suit, the cure in each case being to prise away the trim on the centre pillar and free a small ball bearing at the base. The passenger's seat belt has jammed on subsequent occasions while the retraction of the driver's seat belt is not generally sufficiently energetic to whisk it out of the way.

The windscreen washers have always required too much hard work on their activating button to produce worth while results and on one occasion refused to work at all on normal wipe until attended to. The boot lock grew increasingly reluctant to work unless so much force was used the key was in danger of breaking, but this was attended to at a service and has since been satisfactory.

One sometimes has the feeling that BL spent vast sums on developing a superb motor car then took fright at how much it was going to sell for and indulged in a frenzied bout of penny pinching on its equipment. For general reliability has been exemplary. Even during the weeks of snow the engine started without the slightest hesitation. The car had to remain out of doors overnight because it wasn't able to scale the steep drive up to my garage, so that first thing every morning I had to spend 20 minutes or so to excavate it from beneath a deep covering of snow.

Costs

The Rover averaged 23.33 mpg over the first 12,000 miles, though this figure is biased by the remarkable 27.9 mpg it averaged for the first 4,000 miles that included running-in, and a spell in Finland's low speed limits when it averaged no less than 32 mpg. An average figure these days is much nearer the 20 mpg overall of our road test car. It is not a very economical commuting car when driven normally, since due to its high gearing and considerable weight, it is mostly in third gear. And when not commuting, it is usually going somewhere in a hurry.

The oil consumed, 13.8 pints, does not include any added at services and is fairly heavy. I usually expect to add a pint around every 800 miles, as some of the oil escapes down the valve stems in clouds of blue smoke on starting up first thing. I believe the subsequent introduction of improved oil seals has cured this habit.

The first service cost £3.75 for the oils used. Then came a 3,000 mile service at £13.20 and a 6,000 mile service costing £33.20.

Conclusions

The Rover arrived with a tremendous reputation — Car of the Year and numerous design awards — to replace my much liked Vauxhall Cavalier, and my initial attitude was one of "Well, show me then." Like most BL cars it took a long time to become really free, at least 7,000 miles for the gearbox, but it improved steadily as the miles mounted and is, I think a most successful car and a joy to drive. In spite of the poor reputation gained by this model, I am relieved to say that, so far, mine has proved most reliable.

In brief

Model: Rover 2600
When bought: April, 1978
Total mileage: 12,421
Price when bought: £6,193.43
Price new now: £6,795
Value now: £5,500
Service interval: 3,000 miles

What went wrong

0-6,000 miles: driver's seat belt reluctant to retract, boot trim came unstuck on right hand side, passenger's seat belt jammed in retracted position.

6,000-12,000 miles: boot trim on left hand side came unstuck, Trim under facia locker on passenger's side came unstuck, lamp in locker on drivers side flickering on and off over bumps, windscreen washer not operating on normal "wipe" setting, rattle underneath from handbrake cable, boot lock difficult/impossible to unlock.

What it cost

	£
Petrol (1)	396.06
Servicing (2)	50.15
Tyres (3)	50.93
Road Fund Licence (4)	25.00
Total	522.14

Basic cost per mile = 4.35p
(1) 514.37 gallons of 4 star petrol at average price of 77p a gallon.
(2) See Running costs section for details.
(3) Approximate "cost" of wear of Michelin XVS tyres.
(4) Six month's worth at current road fund licence cost of £50. Full running costs would include insurance (Group 6) and depreciation.

LONG-TERM REPORT

Friday's child?

We thought that story about end-of-the-week cars was just a myth. But experience with our Rover 2600 Automatic leads us to think again

IF YOU EVER buy a car which gives trouble from new, so the old driver's tale went, it was probably built on a Monday or Friday. Then there was the arrival of the Japanese, and their car factories were said to never stop working, so that a car made on Friday was the same as Saturday's, was the same as Sunday's, was the same as Monday's and so on. Maybe the "Friday Car" was a myth after all.

Looking back with the benefit of 20/20 hindsight over 12,000 miles on our long term Rover 2600, we fear that the production line demon is still with us. We accept that one has to fettle a new car in; that a bulb may blow, a glove box hinge require a little oiling; and other minor work may be needed. But are there other Rover 2600s emerging from Jaguar-Rover-Triumph with a tale of woe to match ours? We certainly hope not.

This Rover 2600, with automatic transmission, was bought at the beginning of last summer. However, delivery was delayed by a week or so; the suppliers, New Crown Motors of Dagenham, Essex, had spotted

what they would only describe as a "gearbox problem". Rather than thump our chest and demand to know, revealing the car was to be part of *Autocar's* fleet and proclaiming the divine right of freedom of information for the Press, we accepted the reason for delay with simply the curiosity of a potential owner. In this way, we would be given no special treatment. Eventually, in May, 1978 it arrived, smart in lemon yellow with tan trim. It was to be the regular transport of *Autocar's* Publishing Director Gavin Doyle, who had suffered the slings and arrows of our unreliable Reliant Scimitar GTE.

To his dismay, the back axle emitted a whine on over-run from the moment that the car came into our possession, the rubber tailgate lining was loose and subsequently fell into the luggage area, a window rubber on the driver's door came off, and a useful light which illuminates the stowage area on the driver's side could not be extinguished (very distracting for night driving) unless the bulb was removed. And the car was supplied without a spare set of keys.

Of course, all of these shortcomings could be corrected under BL's Supercover warranty, but it continued to amaze us that a car with such obvious faults (however minor) should reach the customer at all. That they escaped rectification before it was allowed to pass through the Solihull factory gates is surprising, but of more concern, is how it could have passed the comprehensive checklist that the dealer has to certify for the pre-delivery inspection.

At 4,000 miles, the back axle was replaced by New Crown in recognition of the steadily increasing whine. At 4,350 miles the power steering pump failed (a fault which has also beset the company's Rover 3500). Again, rectification was carried out under warranty, and, after 5 months and nearly 5,000 miles, it looked as though the Rover 2600 Automatic had finally shaken off its teething troubles.

Such experiences in the early life of a car can sour the user's trust and confidence in its ability, but no, our Publishing Director quickly came to appreciate the 2600's

practicality and immense driveability, using it to take his family on a touring holiday in France. His faith was rewarded by the car's impeccable behaviour on the trip, transporting him, his wife, son and daughter in their late teens and a mountain of luggage in complete comfort.

Another relatively trouble-free 4,000 miles were put on the clock through the severe winter. The occasional plume of blue smoke had been causing concern for some time. Just before the 2600 was due for its 9,000 mile service this oil burning became much worse. The Rover went to New Crown Motors for its service, and new valve seals were fitted to cure the problem. A leaking seam on the petrol tank required its replacement (with an attendant wait as the dealer did not have one in stock) and attention was paid to a bad earth on the heating element for the rear window. The gear selector bulb was replaced and a new connector was fitted to correct an intermittently functioning heater motor.

A gradual build up in tappet noise prior to the 12,000 miles service was the sole blot on an otherwise clean record sheet after the 9,000 miles repair session. We were told on booking it in for service with Dolphin Square Garages, London SW1, that tappet adjustment was "impossible", and would have to wait until the foreman came back from holiday. They completed the routine 12,000 miles service, replacing the rear brake linings, but not the front disc pads, which had plenty of wear left in them. As we did not want the 2600 off the road for any longer than was absolutely necessary, we took the car to Henly's of Camden Town for the tappet adjustment.

The overhead camshaft design requires more than just a spanner and feeler gauge. The torque settings on the cylinder head have to be checked and adjusted if necessary, and the amount of wear is then determined by feeler gauge. Then the head has to be removed, and shims are added to the bottom of the tappet cup to achieve the correct clearance, which is checked when the head is torqued back down. If the clearance is out, then the whole procedure has to start again. This is a tricky job for the mechanics and financially annoying to the customer as it is time consuming — the shims cost a few pence, but the job

Left: Comfortable roomy interior of the 2600 with seats that provide adequate lateral and lumbar support to take the ache out of long trips. The cloth trim of the seats has stood up well to wear, and the pvc trim of the facia looks as good as when the Rover first arrived

Right and far right: The aerodynamic lines of the SD1 sets the Rover apart from its competitors, and are now a familiar sight on our roads, set to become regarded as classic in their own right

Right: The rear passenger accommodation provides a degree of comfort approaching that of the front seating. Below: Estate car like luggage capacity combined with self-levelling rear suspension make the Rover a really versatile car. The long tailgate is relatively heavy to lift and finding the lock after dark, which is located on the underside of the lip, takes a great deal of fumbling

runs out to between 2-3 hours, and with Henly's labour at £10 an hour, it is not surprising that the bill came to £33.82 including VAT.

Our first 2600 auto

The Rover 2600 is the larger of the two six-cylinder versions of the V8-engined 3500, using the same distinctive SD1 body and giving little away in terms of specification. In five speed manual gearbox form, the 2600 does not lose much on performance, either — 117 mph against the 3500's 123 mph, and little wider acceleration gap to 60 mph of 10.7 sec to the remarkable 8.4 sec achieved by the 3500.

With the installation of an automatic gearbox, it is perhaps not too surprising that the 2600's performance is less lively. Rover use the Borg Warner Type 65 three speed transmission on both the 2600 and 3500. Those who read our feature last month will know that we judged this to be the best automatic of the 10 different types tested. The selection arrangement uses a notched guide plate which allows free movement between Drive and Intermediate, but a

move into Neutral or Low can only be effected by pulling the selector over to the side against a light spring — this safeguards against the unintentional selection of neutral or low gear.

We were also impressed by the smoothness of the up and down changes, whether automatic or manual — you are hardly aware that the transition is taking place. Automatic up changes take place at 35 mph from Low into Intermediate; and at 64 mph from Intermediate into Drive. Manual selection of Low and Intermediate would allow the Rover to reach its red-line speeds in both gears of 56 and 90 mph respectively.

We have not carried out a full Autotest of an automatic Rover 2600, so the figures obtained at our 12,000 mile long term Performance Check are of particular interest.

Not surprisingly we obtained the best 0-60 mph time of 13.8 sec (3.1 sec slower than the manual 2600) by overriding the gearchanges, and top speed was 8 mph slower than the manual 2600 at 109 mph These figures are quite acceptable to the owner who has had little experience of the torquey 3500 or the fast manual 2600, but it gives the

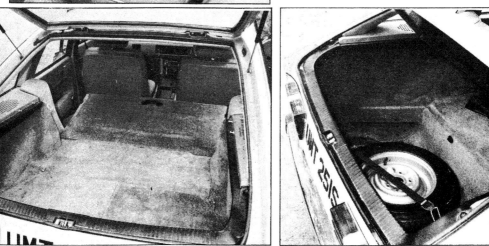

driver more accustomed to the faster models a strange feeling to drive the automatic — almost as if compression has been lost on one cylinder. You can conclude that the Rover is either over-bodied or underpowered, b... is is not really fair; the performance of the automatic 2600 is a good match for other cars in its class.

Well fitted out

The overall effect of the interior makes one feel immediately at home. It is wide and roomy, and the cloth covered seats provide good lumbar and lateral support, wearing well after 12,000 miles' usage. All-round visibility is good, although the steep rake of the wide front and rear screens gives one the impression of a wide angle cinema screen vista; easy to get used to, and all the pillars are narrow enough so as not to restrict vision. One bad point about the two big side mirrors is the manner of adjustment. Their position can be altered from inside the passenger compartment by turning a knob on the inside of each of the blanked-out quarter lights — a good idea in principle, but in practice, it proves difficult to get the fine amount of adjustment needed on the vertical axis without altering the horizontal axis.

The accelerator and large brake pedals were well placed, and the servo-assisted brakes coped well with the lack of engine braking of an automatic. They were on the light side.

The steering wheel is oval. Personal opinions and likes or dislikes vary on the practicality of such a design, but the nature of the power steering softened any strong criticism; high geared, it has only 2.8 turns lock to lock and is unusually responsive, and one of the car's best features.

The instrument console looks like a big black plastic box that has literally been dropped into position on the dashboard. All the gauges are easy to read, and it is good to see battery, oil and temperature gauges with numerical scales instead of the usual vague lettering such as F and C, D and C, H and C, etc.

The overall layout, including buttons, knobs and switches is very clean, though not entirely practical. The manual choke, for example, is operated by a lever which lies flush on the centre console between the front seats, directly beneath the driver's elbow — not the easiest place to reach. Manual chokes are a rarity in this type of car today. The majority now feature an automatic choke, preferable on a car with automatic transmission. Cold starting has never been a problem — even in the depths of last winter.

Tickover when warm is very low indeed at 500 rpm, and we would rather it was raised above this recommended level to aid the getaway from standstill, which is quite sluggish, and can lead to a slight embarrassment when moving off from traffic lights alongside buses and taxis.

As mentioned earlier, the 2600 can take an enormous volume of luggage, and, like the 3500 but unlike the smaller engined 2300, has the self-levelling rear suspension which avoids a nose-up attitude when carrying a lot of weight in the back. Ride is very good with any amount of load. The carrying ability is enhanced further by the hatchback rear and fold down rear seats. One niggle which was also apparent in the 3500 on which we reported long-term is that the removable rear parcel shelf persists in rattling.

The Rover 2600 is a popular candidate for company purchase for middle and senior management. Though it stands up well in specification and performance with foreign competition from manufacturers like Audi, Mercedes and Citroen, ours has fallen down in reliability. That is a mantle of notoriety that it cannot afford to keep. We said when we reported on our early model 3500 that only quality control let it down and we hoped Rover and their dealers would improve. That remains a hope, two years later. □

WHAT THE ROVER 2600 HAS COST

Total 12,000 miles £2,616. **Cost per mile** 21.6p

CONSUMABLE ITEMS	Life in Miles	Unit Cost £	Cost per 12,000 miles £
Fuel: 4-star (gallon)	23.0	1.10	573.91
Oil: topping-up between changes (litre)	1,800	1.00	6.67
Brakes:			
Front pads (Unit cost = set of 4)	15,000	£14.19	11.35
Rear linings (Unit cost = set of 4 on exchange)	10,000	£11.27	9.39
Tyres:			
Front pair	min. 20,000		37.44
Rear pair	min. 25,000		29.95
(Unit cost single tyre)		£31.20	

SERVICE and REPAIRS

Recommended charges for	3,000 miles (optional)	£12.00
service at £8.00	6,000 miles	£28.00
per hour (labour only)	12,000 miles	£32.00
Service costs incurred with our car in past 12,000 miles (inc. oil and materials)		£57.84
Repair costs incurred		£33.82
Total maintenance costs incurred		£91.66

STANDING CHARGES (per year)

Insurance (see note)	£112.85
Tax	£50.00
Depreciation:	
Cost of our car when new	£6,194
Its estimated value today	£4,500
Decline in value over 13 months	£1,694

Note: To put all our cars on equal footing for insurance cost, the figure given above is a typical quotation for a "good risk" driver — with clean record, and car garaged in Oxfordshire, a "middle range" risk area. Full n.c.b. discount has been deducted, as has the saving for £25 excess. The actual figure given is the middle one of five quotations ranging from £109.54 to £121.68. Source: Quotel Motor Insurance Service.

MAXIMUM SPEEDS

Gear	mph	rpm
Top (mean)	109	
(best)	110	
2nd	90	6,000
1st	56	6,000

FUEL CONSUMPTION

Overall mpg

LT 23.0 (12.3 litres / 100km)

ACCELERATION

FROM REST	True mph	Speedo mph	Time (sec)
	30	32.5	5.4
	40	43	7.6
	50	54	10.1
	60	65	13.8
	70	77	17.9
	80	87	23.4
	90	97	33.3
	100	110	
	110	120	

IN EACH GEAR	mph			
	10-30	—	—	3.7
	20-40	—	—	4.5
	30-50	—	—	4.6
	40-60	—	7.6	—
	50-70	12.0	8.6	—
	60-80	14.6	9.9	—
	70-90	19.3	14.3	—
	80-100	27.8	—	—

Standing ¼-mile:
19.5 sec, 73 mph
Standing km:
35.2 sec, 92 mph

SPECIFICATION

ENGINE

Front, rear drive

Cylinders	6 in line
Main bearings	4
Cooling	Water
Fan	Viscous
Bore, mm	81
Stroke, mm	84
Capacity, c.c.	2,597
Valve gear	Ohc
Compression ratio	9.25-to-1
Carburettor	Two SU HS6
Max power	136 bhp (DIN) at 5,000 rpm
Max torque	152 lb. ft. at 5,000 rpm

TRANSMISSION

Gear	Ratio	mph/1,000rpm
3rd	1.00	23.1
2nd	1.45	15.9
1st	2.39	9.7
Final drive gear	Hypoid	
Ratio	3.08	

SUSPENSION

Front—location	MacPherson struts, lower links
springs	Coil
dampers	Telescopic
anti-roll bar	Yes
Rear—location	Live axle, torque tube, Watts linkage
springs	Coil
dampers	Self levelling telescopic
anti-roll bar	No

STEERING

Type	Rack and pinion
Power assistance	Standard
Wheel diameter	15x16in. elliptical

BRAKES

Front	10.15in. dia. disc
Rear	9.0in. dia. drum
Servo	Yes

PRODUCED BY:
Jaguar Rover Triumph Ltd.
Leyland Coventry House
Station Square
Coventry CV1 2FT

Road Test

ROVER V8-S

An impressive all-rounder, refined, versatile and blessed with good road manners that make it an unrivalled long-distance express. Rover's latest version of the long-legged V8 has air conditioning too — an added attraction in the world's best hatchback

FOUR YEARS have already passed since Rover first revealed to an admiring public the all-new 3500 SD1, which went on to scoop up armfuls of design trophies, including the coveted Car of the Year accolade. Since then, with subsequent 2.3 and 2.6-litre six-cylinder versions joining the original V8, the bold and aerodynamic design has become a common sight on British and Continental roads.

In its original 1976 road test, Motor's assessment of the 3500 verged on the ecstatic. But in the intervening years, many new or substantially revised rivals have appeared from the likes of Audi, Ford, Opel and Mercedes; so the Rover's position has shifted from being "the new boy" to almost the old guard in its particular market sector. During

that time its design and specification have remained, superficially at any rate, unchanged, though undoubtedly there has been much underlying detailed development — aimed as much at improving quality control (originally rather suspect) as at keeping the car's dynamic qualities competitive with its rivals. All of which begs the question of whether in 1980 the Rover remains a force to be reckoned with, or whether rising standards have passed it by.

It seemed appropriate to base our re-assessment on the one member of the now four-car range which Motor has not previously tested. Launched in June last year, the V8-S can probably owe its conception to Rover's recent sally on to the potentially lucrative

American market: to sell successfully a luxury car in the US you must be able to offer air conditioning, and the most notable feature that distinguishes the V8-S from the "ordinary" 3500 is that it features air conditioning as standard.

In spite of its usual connotations, the "S" designation in this instance does *not* indicate a more potent or sportier variation on the theme; indeed, if anything the V8-S is a little slower than the 3500, due to the extra weight of superior trim and equipment which, together with the air conditioning, account for the S's £1,693 price premium over the "ordinary" 3500. The most significant extras include headlamp wash/wipe, gold painted alloy wheels, and a (manually operated) sliding steel sunroof. Additionally, the V8-S

is distinguished from its lesser stablemates by a zone-tinted windscreen, black chrome front and rear bumpers, and inside, shag pile carpeting, rear headrests, velour trimmed door panels and cross-ribbed velvet upholstery.

Mechanically, all is essentially as before. The 3.5 litre all-alloy V8 drives through either a five-speed manual or three-speed automatic gearbox, to a live rear axle located by a torque tube, longitudinal radius arms and a transverse Watts linkage. Coil springs are used all round, with self-levelling damper struts at the rear and MacPherson struts at the front with an anti-roll bar. The rack and pinion steering has power assistance, and the front/rear split braking system employs discs at the front and self-adjusting nine inch drums at the rear.

It all adds up to an £11,852 price tag which promotes BL's executive hatchback firmly up-market into a sector populated by many formidable rivals. The most recent of these is the turbocharged five-cylinder Audi 200T, which costs £12,950 with automatic transmission as standard. Also a little dearer and sold only with automatic transmission is the Mercedes 280E, while very similarly priced competition is proved by the Citroen CX Prestige (£11,594) and the Opel Senator 3.0CD (£11,705). Other rivals undercut the Rover slightly, such as the BMW 528i (£10,595), the Granada 2.8i Ghia (£10,377) and the 5-door Saab 900 Turbo (£10,750).

Happily for BL, the Rover as a basic design is still an impressive all-rounder. Refined, versatile and blessed with excellent road manners, it is virtually unrivalled as an economical long-distance express. It is also comfortable and lavishly equipped, though we have reservations about the "S" package's value, given that air conditioning is so rarely needed in the British climate. A few niggles remain, such as hard-to-[read] instruments and the over-long gearing for performance motoring. We are also disappointed and puzzled by the lack of interior legroom for a car of such long wheelbase. Overall, however, it is gratifying to find that the many fine qualities that made the Rover Car of the Year in 1976 remain essentially undiminished four years later.

Although considerably developed since it was first acquired from General Motors in the 'sixties, Rover's pushrod ohv engine remains essentially a "lazy V8". On a 9.35:1 compression ratio and breathing through twin SU carburetters, it produces a modest 155 bhp (DIN) at 5250 rpm, less than its six-cylinder rivals produce on 3 litres or less. However, a meaty torque output of 198 lb ft developed at just 2500 rpm is more impressive, and when these outputs are put to work to power a trim and aerodynamically clean bodyshell, the results are competitive enough.

Our test car lapped MIRA's high speed circuit at 122.0 mph in fourth (119 mph in fifth), which is faster than we have recorded for any rivals at MIRA. Since a significant amount of speed is "scrubbed off" at such speeds by cornering forces through the banked turns, we do not doubt that on a straight level road the Rover would at least match the claimed maximum of 125 mph, a figure which is beaten among our selected rivals only by the BMW's claimed (and equally believable) 129 mph.

Reflecting its slightly greater weight, the V8-S took 9.1 sec for the 0-60 mph sprint, compared to the 3500's 8.9 sec; compared to its rivals, the Rover's standing start acceleration is about average, lagging behind the BMW (8.3 sec) and the Audi (8.6 sec) but bettering the Saab (9.3 sec) and the Mercedes (9.5 sec).

In spite of its exceptionally high gearing, the Rover's low-speed and mid-range pick-up is good. In fourth gear (fifth is strictly a cruising overdrive, and even direct fourth is longer-legged than most rivals' top) the Rover's 30-50 and 50-70 mph times of 7.7 and 7.6 sec respectively better those of any manual-transmission rivals that we've tested (we haven't tested the Saab since it got a five-speed gearbox). Even

in fifth gear the Rover is not, according to the figures, unduly sluggish, taking 10.7 sec each for the 30-50 and 50-70 mph increments.

Subjective impressions, however, belie these figures. So high are all the ratios (at 6000 rpm the intermediates run to 42, 67 and 101 mph) that the Rover is no slingshot off the line, and its long-legged stride gives the impression of sluggishness from low speeds. At 10 mph in second, for example, the engine is barely above idle speed at 900 rpm. Some testers complained of having to drop down not one but two gears when brisk acceleration was called for. However, that's no hardship, for the Rover's slick, positive gearchange — with a particularly easy movement across the dog-leg between fourth and fifth — remains among the best.

In any event the choice of gearing can take much of the credit for the engine's relaxed, fuss-free power delivery — even though the power unit is not especially quiet when revved hard — and the car's exceptionally peaceful high speed cruising capability. With fifth giving 28 mph per 1000 rpm, 70 mph corresponds to a lazy 2500 rpm; even at 100 mph the engine is still turning over at only 3550 rpm.

Economy also benefits, particularly when cruising on the open road: steady speed figures like 36.9 mpg at 40 mph, 26.4 at 70 and 21.4 mpg at 90 mph help produce a computed touring figure of 23.6 mpg, exactly the same as that for the 1976 3500 test car. But while this remains a good result for a car of the Rover's size and speed — driving moderately the average owner should expect about 25 mpg — improvements among the opposition mean that it is no longer the exceptional result that it was in 1976. Overall the V8-S returned 18.9 mpg, a competitive result but a long way down on the 1976 car's 22.5 mpg, for which the increased weight and the power absorbed by the air conditioning must take some of the blame. It should be pointed out, however, that a substantial proportion of the V8-S's mileage was covered on the Continent, heavily

Well-shaped seats (above, left) give driving comfort, though tall folk may find themselves with insufficient legroom. (Above, right) rear accommodation is limited for a car of this size, especially with the front seats well back.

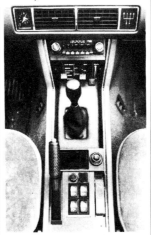

Clear dial markings make all the instruments easy to read (above) though the wheel may shroud them. Well-placed console controls include, unusually, a choke lever.

laden and at higher cruising speeds than are possible in this country. On the basis of the touring figure, the 14.5 gallon tank allows a maximum range of around 340 miles between refills.

At first the Rover V8-S's sharp, exceptionally direct steering can be a trifle disconcerting, for until you learn the necessary smoothness of touch you are liable to take corners somewhat jerkily. With familiarity, however, you soon appreciate that its power-assisted rack and pinion mechanism is

one of the best around — not as light as some at parking speeds, but ideally weighted on the move. The behaviour of the chassis is equally good; when cornered fast the Rover is little affected by mid-corner bumps, maintains an essentially neutral balance up to very high cornering forces, and is unlikely to lose its poise even under such extreme provocation as hard braking in mid-bend. The brakes performed faultlessly under all conditions.

Most of our testers did feel, though, that the handling seemed a little softer and that the car leaned more in hard cornering than before, but by the same token the ride — never poor — had been improved. In particular, the V8-S proved much more supple over small bumps at suburban speeds, and overall the Rover now rides at least as well as most of its independently sprung rivals. Only the occasional tendency to jar over transverse ridges, particularly under acceleration, remains to remind you that the Rover has a live rear axle.

One effect of the softer suspension is that the car tends to float over bumps taken at high speed, though this characteristic is only obtrusive when the car is heavily laden. More importantly, however, the V8-S is disconcertingly sensitive to cross winds at high speed, detracting from the car's otherwise superb cruising ability. No doubt the addition of spoilers front and rear would afford an easy solution.

A somewhat unexpected deficiency is the Rover's disappointingly limited passenger accommodation, which is significantly inferior to that of the original 3500 of 1976. You don't need to be

continued over

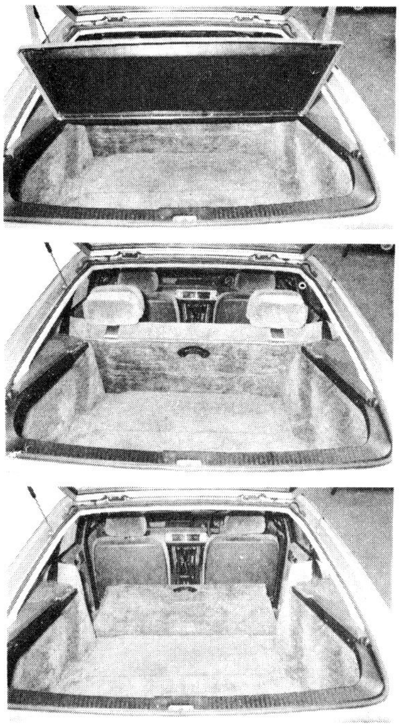

Big; bigger; biggest! The generous boot (top) is expanded by removal of the parcel shelf (centre), and extended almost to estate proportions when the rear seat is folded (bottom)

unusually tall to find yourself short of leg and headroom at the wheel, and with the front seats at full travel there's a lack of knee-room in the rear which is aggravated by insufficient foot-room beneath the front seats for those with largish feet. The boot, however, is of a reasonable size, and the Rover scores over most rivals with its hatchback and folding rear seat, which provide it with a semi-estate car facility. There's an exceptional amount of space for oddments in the 'shin bins' in the front footwells and in the tray set into the top of the facia.

Unless they're tall enough for head- and leg-room to be a problem, most drivers should be able to make themselves very comfortable, for the wheel itself is adjustable for reach and height, the other major controls are well placed, and the comfortably sprung seat is well shaped, though some drivers would have liked a little more under-thigh support. The column stalks — horn/dip/flash/indicators on the right, wash/wipe on the left — work well, and the lights master switch, although not easily visible, is easily found by touch in its position on the steering column. The choke, unusually, is by a lever on the transmission tunnel, while most of the minor electrical switches are closely grouped at the right hand end of the instrument pod, where it can be a fumble to find the right one at night.

The instruments are deeply recessed into their rectangular housing, where the tops of the six dials are shrouded from view of tall drivers, and depending on the position at which it is set the wheel may partly obscure some of the minor gauges. The latter — for battery voltage, fuel level, oil pressure and water temperature — are grouped together to the left, with the speedo and tachometer immediately facing the driver. All the dials are clearly calibrated and well lit at night.

Exceptionally powerful halogen headlamps make light work of night driving and the wipers (two constant speeds and intermittent wipe) work well in most circumstances, though even their fast speed is hopelessly inadequate for a torrential downpour, and on our test car they tended to lift at over 90 mph. On the move there are no problematic blind spots, but some drivers commented that the car felt a lot wider than it actually is. In tight spaces the way the extremities of the car drop away out of sight make parking manoeuvres difficult to judge, though the twin internally adjustable door mirrors provide some compensation. The lack of a rear wash/wipe is only a problem after the car has been standing in the rain, and when moving at very low speeds. At over 30 mph, the screen keeps itself admirably clear of rain and road filth.

There are two bonuses afforded by the air conditioning: the ability of its dehumidifier to help prevent internal misting up in heavy rain; and the ability to overcome the heating of the ventilator ducts when the car has been standing for some time. Otherwise we have reservations about the air conditioning's value: not because it doesn't work well — in fact we found it admirably controllable and flexible — but because the Rover's normal heating and ventilation are so good, and the times when you are likely to need air conditioning in this country are so rare. The face-level vents provide copious quantities of air whether the air conditioning is on or not, and the heating is powerful and responsive to its controls.

Few cars are as relaxed and peaceful as the Rover is at high cruising speeds, thanks not only to the high gearing, but also the suppression of wind noise, which is much better than in earlier cars. The engine is only ever noticeable under hard acceleration, particularly over 5000 rpm, though one rarely uses such high revs in practice. Apart from occasional thumping over broken surfaces, road noise is generally well suppressed.

If our test car was anything to go by, Rover have now achieved the standard of finish that the excellence of the basic design deserves. The car's structure feels rattle-free, and it looks good with metallic paint and gold-painted alloy wheels. The shag pile carpet is positively luxurious, and velvety cloth trim is used extensively for the seat facings and door panels and headlining.

There are only a very few things missing from the Rover's equipment list that some other cars do have — height/tilt adjustment for the driver's seat cushion, and a rear screen wiper, being the notable ones. Quite apart from the air conditioning, headlamp wash/wipe, and sliding steel sunroof (which is manually operated by a single pull of the combined handle/release lever) which are part of the 'S' package, the 'basic' 3500 Rover is already extremely well equipped, with such items as adjustable steering, alloy wheels, mudflaps, centralised door locking, electric windows, a radio stereo cassette player, halogen headlamps and front fog lamps, self levelling suspension, a tachometer, and internally adjustable door mirrors.

MOTOR ROAD TEST NO 28/80 ● ROVER V8-S

PERFORMANCE

CONDITIONS

Weather	Wind 5-15 mph
Temperature	55°F
Barometer	29.6 in Hg
Surface	Dry tarmacadam

MAXIMUM SPEEDS

	mph	kph
Banked Circuit	122.0	196.3
Best ¼ mile	125.0	201.1
Terminal Speeds:		
at ¼ mile	81	130
at kilometre	130	166
Speed in gears (at 6000 rpm):		
1st	42	68
2nd	67	108
3rd	101	163

ACCELERATION FROM REST

mph	sec	kph	sec
0-30	3.1	0-40	2.4
0-40	4.9	0-60	4.4
0-50	6.9	0-80	6.9
0-60	9.1	0-100	9.9
0-70	12.7	0-120	14.3
0-80	16.2	0-140	19.0
0-90	20.3	0-160	28.0
0-100	28.3		
Stand'g ¼	16.6	Stand'g km	30.8

ACCELERATION IN TOP

mph	sec	kph	sec
20-40	11.7	40-60	7.2
30-50	10.7	60-80	6.3
40-60	10.7	80-100	7.0
50-70	10.7	100-120	7.0
60-80	11.5	120-140	8.7
70-90	13.5		
80-100	17.7		

ACCELERATION IN 4TH

mph	sec	kph	sec
20-40	8.5	40-60	5.3
30-50	7.7	60-80	4.6
40-60	7.5	80-100	4.8
50-70	7.6	100-120	5.0
60-80	8.4	120-140	6.2
70-90	9.8	140-160	8.3
80-100	12.3		

FUEL CONSUMPTION

Touring*	23.6 mpg 12.0 litres/100 km
Overall	18.9 mpg 15.0 litres/100 km
Govt tests	16.2 mpg (urban) 36.3 mpg (56 mph) 27.9 mpg (75 mph)

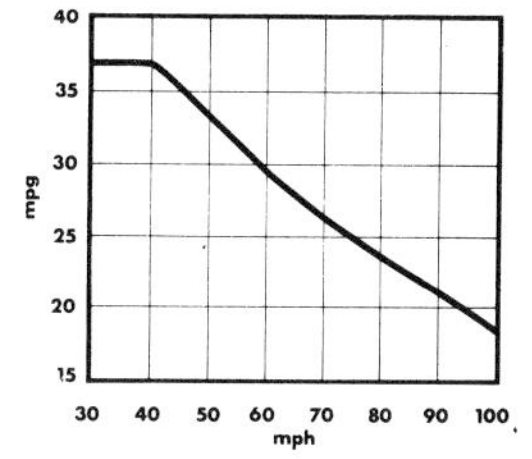

Fuel grade	97 octane 4 star rating
Tank capacity	14.5 galls 66 litres
Max range	342 miles 551 km
Test distance	2475 miles 3982 km

*Consumption midway between 30 mph and maximum less 5 per cent for acceleration.

NOISE

	dBA	Motor rating
30 mph	61	8.5
50 mph	65	11
70 mph	72	18
Max revs in 2nd	80	32

*A rating where 1 = 30 dBA and 100 = 96 dBA, and where double the number means double the loudness

SPEEDOMETER (mph)

Speedo	30	40	50	60	70	80	90	100
True mph	28	38	48	58	67	76	86	95

Distance recorder: 3.4 per cent fast

WEIGHT

	cwt	kg
Unladen weight*	27.0	1372
Weight as tested	30.7	1560

*with fuel for approx 50 miles

Performance tests carried out by Motor's staff at the Motor Industry Research Association proving ground, Lindley.

Test Data: World Copyright reserved; no unauthorised reproduction in whole or part.

GENERAL SPECIFICATION

ENGINE

Cylinders	V8
Capacity	3528 cc (215.1 cu in)
Bore/stroke	88.9/71.1 mm (3.50/2.80 in)
Cooling	Water
Block	Light alloy
Head	Light alloy
Valves	Pushrod ohv
Cam drive	Chain
Compression	9.35:1
Carburetter	Twin SU HIF6 sidedraught
Bearings	5 main
Max power	155 bhp (DIN) at 5250 rpm
Max torque	198 lb ft (DIN) at 2500 rpm

TRANSMISSION

Type	5-speed manual,
Clutch dia	9.5 in
Actuation	Hydraulic
Internal ratios and mph/1000 rpm	
Top	0.833:1/28.1
4th	1.000:1/23.4
3rd	1.396:1/16.8
2nd	2.087:1/11.2
1st	3.321:1/7.0
Rev	3.428:1
Final drive	3.08:1

BODY/CHASSIS

Construction	Unitary; steel
Protection	Electrophoretic primer; full undersealant, ventilated sills; zinc coated outer sill panels

SUSPENSION

Front	Independent by MacPherson struts, and lower wi bones formed by tra verse arm and anti-roll bar; coil springs.
Rear	Live axle located by torque tube, Watts linkage and radius arms; coil springs; selfenergising, self-levelling damper struts.

STEERING

Type	Rack and pinion
Assistance	Yes

BRAKES

Front	10.2 in dia discs
Rear	9.0 in dia drums
Park	On rear
Servo	Yes
Circuit	Split front/rear
Rear valve	Yes
Adjustment	Automatic

WHEELS/TYRES

Type	Alloy, 6J × 14 in
Tyres	195/70 HR 14
Pressures	26/26 psi F/R (normal) 26/30 psi F/R (full load)

ELECTRICAL

Battery	12V, 66 Ah
Earth	Negative
Generator	Alternator
Fuses	11
Headlights	
type	Halogen
dip	110 W total
main	120 W total

Make: Rover
Model: V8-S
Maker: Jaguar Rover Triumph Ltd, Browns Lane, Allesley, Coventry CV5 9DR
Price: £9,513.00 plus £792.75 Car Tax plua £1,545.86 VAT equals £11,851.61 Total

The Rivals

Other possible rivals include the Citroen CX Prestige (£11,594), Peugeot 604 TI (£10,205), Vauxhall Royale (£10,524), Saab 900 Turbo (£10,750) and Volvo 264GLE (£10,095)

ROVER V8-S £11,852

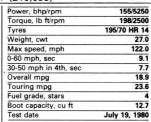

Power, bhp/rpm	155/5250
Torque, lb ft/rpm	198/2500
Tyres	195/70 HR 14
Weight, cwt	27.0
Max speed, mph	122.0
0-60 mph, sec	9.1
30-50 mph in 4th, sec	7.7
Overall mpg	18.9
Touring mpg	23.6
Fuel grade, stars	4
Boot capacity, cu ft	12.7
Test date	July 19, 1980

Most plush of Rover's SD1 range. Mechanically identical (with choice of 5-speed manual or 3-speed auto box) to ordinary 3500 but with different trim, air conditioning and sliding roof. Superb handling car with a ride that's now a match for most fully independent rivals. Long-legged gearing gives outstanding cruising and reasonable economy. A great driver's car.

AUDI 200T £12,950

Power, bhp/rpm	170/5300
Torque, lb ft/rpm	195/3300
Tyres	205/60 HR15
Weight, cwt	24.8
Max speed, mph	119.7
0-60 mph, sec	8.6
30-50 mph in kickdown, sec	3.3
Overall mpg	17.8
Touring mpg	—
Fuel grade, stars	4
Boot capacity, cu ft	14.0
Test date	June 21, 1980

Audi's first turbocharged car, based on the five-cylinder 100 5E but with bigger brakes, stiffer suspension and a lavish specification. UK versions will be mostly autos, in which form 200 is responsive, smooth and has very fast acceleration. Handling is outstanding, as is high-speed stability, particularly over bumps. Jiggly ride but generally comfortable and quiet. A superb cross-country express.

BMW 528i £10,595

Power, bhp/rpm	184/5800
Torque, lb ft/rpm	177/4200
Tyres	195/70 HR 14
Weight, cwt	27.6
Max speed, mph	129
0-60 mph, sec	8.3
30-50 mph in 4th, sec	9.1
Overall mpg	17.9
Touring mpg	—
Fuel grade, stars	4
Boot capacity, cu ft	13.0
Test date	December 31, 1977

Perhaps the best of all the BMWs with its handsome, roomy, 5-Series body, comfortable ride and superb handling. Top-gear acceleration is only fair, but in all other respects the fuel-injected engine gives excellent performance including a maximum speed approaching 130 mph. Comfortable seat and control layout, well-designed instruments, but indifferent heating and ventilation. Tested as 4-speed; now available as 5-speed at extra cost.

FORD GRANADA 2.8i GHIA £10,377

Power, bhp/rpm	160/5700
Torque, lb ft/rpm	162/4300
Tyres	190/65 HR 390
Weight, cwt	26.1
Max speed, mph	117.4
0-60 mph, sec	9.0
30-50 mph in 4th, sec	9.3
Overall mpg	20.4
Touring mpg	—
Fuel grade, stars	4
Boot capacity, cu ft	13.2
Test date	September 17, 1977
Performance figs for 2.8iS manual	

Most expensive, luxury version of Ford's Granada saloon, though tested by us in similar iS manual form, with good performance though at the expense of low-speed torque. Good ride, handling and roadholding, and generally very refined. Comfortable, plush interior, very roomy, and very well equipped — even a sunroof is standard. Brakes don't inspire confidence under hard use, and steering lacks feel.

MERCEDES 280E £12,775

Power, bhp/rpm	185/5800
Torque, lb ft/rpm	177/4500
Tyres	195/70 HR 14
Weight, cwt	32.1
Max speed, mph	117.7
0-60 mph, sec	9.5
30-50 mph in kickdown, sec	4.8
Overall mpg	19.0
Touring mpg	—
Fuel grade, stars	4
Boot capacity, cu ft	14.2
Test date (Estate)	June 9, 1979

Mercedes' "small" saloon in its most powerful form, with excellent performance and reasonable economy from delightfully smooth engine and four speed automatic combination, despite latter's reluctant part-throttle kickdown. Outstandingly surefooted handling, reasonable ride and refinement. All traditional Mercedes virtues — engineering integrity and attention to detail. We haven't tested the saloon since recent power increase, so quote estate figures.

OPEL SENATOR 3.0CD £11,705

Power, bhp/rpm	180/5800
Torque, lb ft/rpm	183/4200-4800
Tyres	195/70 HR 14
Weight, cwt	27.3
Max speed, mph	125 (estimated)
0-60 mph, sec	9.0
30-50 mph in kickdown, sec	3.2
Overall mpg	18.0
Touring mpg	—
Fuel grade, stars	4
Boot capacity, cu ft	14.2
Test date	July 19, 1980
(figures from long-term test car)	

Opel's prestige saloon combines refinement and comfort with brisk performance. Smooth-changing automatic gearbox (manual available to special order), excellent ride and handling, good brakes; luxurious, lavishly equipped, though not as spacious as some rivals. Good heating, excellent ventilation, huge boot. Some aspects of the interior finish are not to our taste, and the engine is a bit noisy at some speeds. Plenty of appeal for the sporty driver.

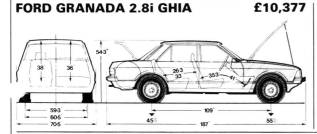

I'LL GO NO MORE A-ROVERING

With over 50,000 miles recorded, Philip Turner's Rover 2600 no longer had the body beautiful: but at heart it was still young

My Rover 2600 had covered 53,913 miles when on a Tuesday in May I parked it on the roof at Surrey House and closed the driver's door behind me for the last time. On the run down the M1 from Birmingham that morning it had shown very few signs of old age so far as its performance and handling ere concerned. Eager as ever, it ould gradually increase speed if left to its own devices and was just as happy at 90 mph as it was at a legal 70 — if not more so . . .

When I last reported on the Rover in our December 13, 1980 issue, it had covered 46,900 miles, and had therefore reached maturity. It had been remarkably trouble-free, troubles being confined to trim coming unstuck, handbrake cables that tended to seize in the "on" position, though never enough to lock the brakes on so that driving was impossible, and a leak in the seal round the massive hatchback rear window that time and again turned the spare wheel well under the boot floor into a fair-sized swimming pool. The leak was eventually cured, but then one morning I found a large pool on the garage floor underneath the front of the car. The cause was eventually traced to a leaking water pump and dealt with, but in November of last year the cooling system again began losing its water, and this was found to be due to a leak from the head gasket at the rear of the block. First sign of trouble in this direction was a lack of heat from the heater, rather than any indication of overheating from the temperature gauge. Maybe the gasket had suffered from local overheating when the car had previously lost coolant from the leaking water pump. The leaking head gasket, which did not affect the performance or running of the engine, was replaced and all was well.

Early in January, as I was returning from an evening meeting in darkest Birmingham, the clutch became more and more reluctant to disengage as the journey progressed until finally it would do so only after energetic pumping of the clutch pedal. A little experimenting showed that clutchless upward and downward gear changes were possible, but traffic lights at red were a real problem.

A visit to my ever helpful Rover dealers the following morning showed that the clutch master cylinder was leaking away its fluid at a great rate, so this component was replaced. This was at just under the 50,000-mile mark, and the car was also given a 6,000-mile service for which it was about due. During this service, the somewhat corroded exhaust tailpipe was replaced, new front brake pads were fitted, and the offside rear handbrake cable quadrant was freed yet again.

After this, the Rover continued to run with no further troubles at all for the next three thousand miles or so up to the time when I parted with it, the only time it returned to the dealers being to take its MOT test, which it passed with flying colours.

If the mechanical state of the Rover was very sound when I parted with it, the state of the body was not so satisfactory. Although my Rover was not one of the early cars, the company had by no means tamed its new paint plant at Solihull when my 2600 was delivered, and towards the end of its time in my hands some rather odd looking areas could be seen on close inspection of the doors. Rust, too, was becoming evident ahead of the rear wheel arches and on the rear quarter above the right rear wheel arch.

I always thought the interior of the Rover was somewhat of a letdown, and the rather cheap-looking carpeting had begun to wear badly in the front compartment, especially on the driver's side. I never came to like the box of instruments plonked down on top of the facia, and was disappointed that the doors closed with a clang rather than with a clunk.

The body, in fact, was the worst feature of the Rover. It was indeed a success from a styling point of view — I still recall how it emptied a pottery of its design staff in Finland, who poured out to admire "the best looking car we've seen for a very long time."

But from a practical point of view there just was not enough passenger room inside this very large car, and with that massive nose falling away out of sight and a rear hatchback that was steeply sloped and ended in a deep sill it was by no means an easy car to extract from a congested car park.

I still think the original idea of selling the 2600 Rover as a Triumph sports saloon was the right one, for in its performance, its handling and its whole general character the 2600 is much nearer to being a sports saloon than normal dull executive transport. In which case, nobody would have complained about the lack of room in the body or the fair amount of noise from the engine.

Probably it was because the Rover was at heart a sports saloon was the reason why I liked it so much. It was indeed a real driver's car which seemed to delight in being driven hard and which so repaid a driver prepared to make full use of its gearbox, its handling and its performance.

IN BRIEF
Model: Rover 2600
When bought: April, 1978
Total mileage: 53,913
Price when bought: £6,193
Price now: £9,757 (improved model)
Overall mpg: 21.12

Faults and failures
0-6,000 miles: driver's seat belt reluctant to retract, boot trim unstuck on righthand side, passenger's seat belt jammed in retracted position.
6,000-12,000 miles: Boot trim on lefthand side came unstuck, trim under facia locker on passenger's side unstuck, lamp in locker on driver's side flickering on and off over bumps, windscreen washer not operating on normal "wipe" setting, rattle underneath from handbrake cable, boot lock difficult, impossible to unlock.
12,000-24,000 miles Left rear tyre punctured, water leak into boot — tailgate seal replaced without effecting complete cure, front brake pads replaced.
24,000-30,000 miles: Handbrake cable to right rear wheel seized and replaced, fuel gauge read "full" for a time when tank half empty but recovered, kick strip on sill beneath driver's door broken and replaced. Boot trim on lefthand side unstuck again.
30,000-40,000 miles: Bulb failed in left outer headlamp and replaced. Right rear tyre flat so replaced by spare and subsequently the three other tyres replaced by new ones Left rear handbrake cable seizing. Slight leak from power steering pump attended to. Boot seal replaced and boot no longer leaks. Intermittent operation of reversing lamps attended to at 6,000-mile service.
40,000-46,000 miles: Handbrake cable again tending to seize, so attended to and rear brakes relined plus attention to fuel gauge which persistently registered "full." All at 12,000-mile service Leak from water pump attended to.
46,000-54,000 miles: Cylinder head gasket replaced, exhaust tail pipe replaced, front brake pads replaced, handbrake cable again freed, leaking clutch master cylinder replaced.

continued over

SIGNING OFF; MOTOR'S OLD STAGERS

RoadTest

ROVER 2000

The Rover 2000 is reborn in SDI form: bad news for the 2-litre Ford Granada?

WHEN THE Rover 3500 SD1 was launched seven years ago it was a sensation. Where contemporary executive cars contrived to be as conservative as their typical owners, the David Bache-styled Rover looked like a five-door Ferrari Daytona. Its combination of pace, handling and ultra long-legged cruising outranked anything else at the price (then £4,750), and in our 1976 road test it scored an almost unprecedented eight maximum five-star category ratings. A success story in the making, Europe's largest hatchback went on to win a cupboardful of design trophies, including the much ballyhooed Car of the Year award.

Depressingly, the Rover has never achieved the success indicated by its early acclaim. Certainly, the introduction of 2.3 and 2.6-litre six cylinder versions broadened the SD1's appeal and subsequent small revisions and detail changes fine-tuned it to cus-

tomer demands — but such measures were overshadowed by build quality horror stories that stuck to the Rover reputation more tenaciously than the most bloodthirsty of leeches. The sudden and dramatic contraction of the big car market in the late 'seventies — and the higher percentage of new or substantially revised models from the likes of Audi, Ford, Opel and Mercedes competing in it — dealt a further body blow to sales, a situation BL could do little to counter at a time when the struggle for mere survival was all consuming.

But now they can, and have. In January, the company announced an extensive package of revisions and improvements to an expanded Rover range. The more important changes include a new tailgate window extended downward by six inches for better rearward visibility; front spoilers (for all models except the new 2000

and basic 2300) to improve stability at high speed; the adoption of automatic chokes on all models and of five-speed gearboxes for all manual transmission models; a redesigned instrument binnacle; a series of measures which extend servicing intervals and reduce ownership costs; and the addition of walnut trim panels to the more expensive models. All these should capitalise on what BL claim to be a gradual upswing in Rover's market share — from 12.6 per cent in 1980 to 15.1 per cent in 1981, compared with a fall, for the Ford Granada, from 19.2 per cent to 14.2 per cent, according to BL.

The Vanden Plas, 3500 SE, 2600 S, 2300 S and 2300 model structure remains the same, but is extended at its base by the addition of a new two-litre car powered by the four-cylinder O-series engine, thus reviving the famous Rover 2000 model name. Since some 75 per cent of Rover sales have, hitherto, been to company fleets, it is hoped that the new two-litre car will appeal to private buyers and, therefore, play an important part in improving the market penetration of the range. We test it here.

Apart from its engine, the 2000 differs little, mechanically, from its faster stablemates or, indeed, the superseded models. The engine, of course, is front mounted and drives to a live rear axle located longitudinally by a torque

tube and radius arms, and laterally by a Watt's linkage. As before, there is a MacPherson strut suspension system at the front with coil springs and an anti-roll bar, which works in conjunction with rack and pinion steering, power assisted on our test car but not as standard.

At £7,450, the 2000 is £520 cheaper than the basic 2300 and around half the price of the top-line Vanden Plas (£14,480). More significantly, however, the 2000's price takes the Rover name down market to do battle with the lesser Ford Granadas (like the £7,210 2.0 L and the £7,999 2.3 L) and their traditional rivals. These include the Opel Rekord 2.0S Berlina (£7,484), the Talbot Tagora 2.2 GL 5-speed (£7,739) and the Volvo 244 DL with overdrive (£7,359), not forgetting the Vanden Plas version of BL's new Ambassador 2.0 (£7,765).

The power output of the Rover's 1994 cc four-cylinder single overhead camshaft O-series engine, which is fitted with two SU HIF 44 carburetters, is 101 bhp (DIN) at 5250 rpm. This compares with 92 bhp at 4900 rpm for the same engine breathing through a single SU, as it does in the two-litre Morris Ital. There's more torque, too — 120 lb ft at 3250 for the Rover against 114 lb ft at 2750 rpm for the Ital. The compression ratio is 9.0:1.

At 25.5 cwt, the four-cylinder model

is some 0.2 cwt lighter than the last six-cylinder 2300 we tested, but still by no means the featherweight of its class. There is little doubt that Rover have taken a gamble by pairing the far from muscular two-litre O-series unit with the large SD1 body, but the resulting package isn't as sluggish as one might expect. On the other hand, the performance isn't very good for the price.

The maximum speed, achieved in fourth gear, is 102.5 mph, close enough to the claimed 104 mph to satisfy us that given the calm conditions denied our test session the Rover would do just that; the class norm is around 105 mph. The acceleration, however, is mediocre with 60 mph being reached from rest in 12.4 sec (0.1 sec improvement on Rover's claim), which puts the Rover near the bottom of the class, a second or more adrift of the Ford, Opel and Talbot. Nor is the Rover strong on low and mid-range pulling power. In a lighter and lower geared car, 120 lb ft of torque would guarantee good flexibility, but in the Rover it means that, even in fourth, it takes 11.3 sec and 12.6 sec to cover the 30-50 mph and 50-70 mph increments, respectively. Change up into fifth and the same increments take a yawning 18.7 sec and 20.2 sec.

It's just as well, therefore, that changing gear in the Rover is no chore. The gearchange isn't the fastest or lightest around but its short throw action is precise and positive with an easy dog-leg movement into fifth. The medium weight clutch takes up the drive progressively, but the gearbox whines in the lower gears, accompanying the disappointingly harsh and agricultural sound of the engine when extended. To be fair, though, the engine is reasonably smooth and free from significant boom periods and, in gentle driving, seldom draws attention to itself. Moreover, cruising at 70-90 mph is very relaxed, fifth gear giving no less than 23.2 mph per 1000 rpm. The intermediate ratios are quite closely spaced, with no noticeable gaps, per-

Above left: front seats are big, well padded and very comfortable. Above right: rear legroom remains unexceptional by the standards of the big car class, however

Facia is stylish and chunky and incorporates an immense amount of stowage space for oddments

mitting maxima of 33, 53 and 79 mph.

Despite BL's claims, a large car powered by a comparatively small engine is seldom a recipe for good economy and the Rover 2000 proves the point. Its overall consumption of 23.3 mpg, as ever the result of hard driving, is about average for the class, though bettered by the faster Talbot (24.3 mpg). The touring consumption of 26.9 mpg (still nothing special even allowing for the poor testing conditions) better indicates what most owners should be able to achieve and allows a practical range of around 350 miles on a 14.5 gallon tankful of four-star petrol.

As always, the Rover's power steering is exceptionally quick and direct, demanding greater than usual sensitivity of touch to conduct the car smoothly through a corner. But that of our test car was judged to be too light for good feel, loss of grip at the front

The new instruments are generally clear and effective, but the speedo calibrations are too closely packed and confuse the eye

providing no discernible lightening of steering weight. The behaviour of the chassis, however, remains excellent. When cornered hard on bumpy roads, the Rover exhibits remarkable composure for a live-axled car, and it refuses to be upset by lifting off the throttle or even under such extreme provocation as hard braking in mid-bend.

Most of our testers did feel though, that the cornering balance has been pushed still further towards understeer — in contrast to the early cars' almost neutral handling attitude — and that body lean in tight, fast bends is now considerable. But the softer handling is to the good of ride comfort which, although still jiggly over small bumps around the suburbs, smooths out very well at speed, coping competently with most types of road surface, though the occasional tendency to jar over transverse ridges leaves you in no doubt

continued over

that the Rover has a live rear axle. The brakes are powerful but would benefit from being more progressive.

Despite a claimed small increase in legroom, the Rover is not a particularly roomy car. A continuing source of puzzlement to us is why the original 3500 was more spacious than all subsequent SD1 models. As things are, tall drivers will still find themselves short of legroom (though, without the factory fitted sunroof option headroom is adequate), and with the front seats pushed right back, kneeroom in the rear remains at a premium. The luggage area is a decent size, however, and the Rover scores over most other rivals with its hatchback and folding rear seat, not to mention the exceptional amount of stowage for oddments provided by the "shin-bins" in the front footwells and the shelf set into the top of the facia.

Apart from its limited legroom for tall drivers (who are forced to adopt a slightly knees-up posture at the wheel), the Rover's driving position is fine, with a good pedal layout and a steering wheel which (although too big) is adjustable for reach and height. The other major controls are well placed, but the location of some minor push-push switches takes some learning. The seats, although lacking the adjustable lumbar support of dearer models in the range, are generously dimensioned, well padded and very comfortable. The column stalks — horn/dip-flash/winkers on the right, wash/wipe on the left — work well.

The larger tailgate window aids rearward visibility, but it still isn't possible easily to judge where the back of the car ends or, come to that, where the sloping nose begins. Otherwise, there are no serious blind spots and the mirrors on both doors provide a wide field of view behind. At night, the headlamps give an exceptionally powerful and well defined spread of light and, in dirty weather, the wash-wipe systems do a good job; the intermittent facility for the rear is a welcome sophistication.

The new-style instrument binnacle and the redesigned instruments contained therein are not only a big improvement over the old "take-away" pod, but very good by absolute standards. Only the densely-packed markings on the speedometer in any way detract from the display's clarity. The matching quadrant-shaped speedometer and rev counter flank a block of warning lights and telltales, all of which are visible through the steering wheel, and slightly out of line of sight are three minor dials providing information on

fuel level, coolant temperature and oil pressure.

Output from the Rover's heater is powerful and well diffused. A fine degree of control is provided by the simple, easy action slides, though the fan speed selector can be fiddly. The ventilation is equally effective being independent of the heater and fan boostable. Easy to regulate for flow and direction, the system can give a comfortably cool atmosphere at face level and warm footwells at the same time.

Above about 4000 rpm, the Rover's engine, as already discussed, sounds unpleasantly harsh and strained though this is deceptive since our noise measurements show the Rover to be less noisy than average. Both road roar and wind noise are well suppressed.

What is undeniable is that the Rover's interior, even in base 2000 form, exudes an air of luxury. The velour-trimmed seats and thick carpets *are* impressive, as is the fact that the instrumentation is exactly the same as that of the top-of-the-range Vanden Plas. The overall effect is both plush and tasteful. We must be more critical, however, of the interior build quality. While the test car was with us there was a constant, and annoying, creaking from the area of the facia. Worse still both a plastic door lock surround and seat recline handwheel fell off. Externally, the well-applied paintwork and snug panel fit are more encouraging, though the move towards bright trim detailing was less well liked by our testers.

The list of standard equipment on the Rover 2000 contains most creature comforts which might be expected for the price, including a push-button radio, "velvet" seat trim, multi-adjustable steering, a laminated windscreen, twin remote control door mirrors and a digital clock with stop watch facility.

A smarter and more effective Rover range is something of which we wholeheartedly approve. Europe's biggest and best hatchback is a commodity BL, understandably, should want to preserve. However, we find the 2000 a difficult car to come to terms with. Undoubtedly an attractive alternative to the four-cylinder Ford Granada and, indeed, a likeable car in its own right, the crudeness of its engine seems at odds with standards of refinement and luxury attained by the rest of its design. With neither performance nor economy to commend it, we can think of no good reason for not spending another £500 for the six-cylinder 2300.

O-series "four" looks lost in an engine bay designed to take a V8, but there's plenty of space to get at service items

MOTOR ROAD TEST NO 18/82 ●
ROVER 2000

PERFORMANCE

WEATHER CONDITIONS

Wind	10-30 mph
Temperature	39°F/4°C
Barometer	29.9 in Hg
Surface	Dry tarmacadam

MAXIMUM SPEEDS

	mph	kph
Banked Circuit	102.5	164.9
Best ¼ mile	108.4	174.4
Terminal Speeds:		
at ¼ mile	74	119
at kilometre	89	143
Speeds in gears (at 6000 rpm):		
1st	33	53
2nd	53	85
3rd	79	127

ACCELERATION FROM REST

mph	sec	kph	sec
0-30	4.0	0-40	3.0
0-40	6.3	0-60	5.5
0-50	8.8	0-80	8.7
0-60	12.4	0-100	13.3
0-70	16.9	0-120	19.6
0-80	23.4	0-140	30.9
Stand'g ¼	18.9	Stand'g km	35.0

ACCELERATION IN TOP

mph	sec	kph	sec
20-40	19.2	40-60	11.1
30-50	18.7	60-80	10.6
40-60	18.9	80-100	10.9
50-70	20.2	100-120	12.9

ACCELERATION IN 4th

mph	sec	kph	sec
20-40	11.6	40-60	7.1
30-50	11.3	60-80	7.0
40-60	11.4	80-100	6.7
50-70	12.6	100-120	8.7
60-80	14.7		

FUEL CONSUMPTION

Touring*	26.9 mpg
	10.5 litres/100 km
Overall	23.3 mpg
	12.1 litres/100km
Govt tests	23.9 mpg (urban)
	42.6 mpg (56 mph)
	32.7 mpg (75 mph)
Fuel grade	9 octane
	4 star rating

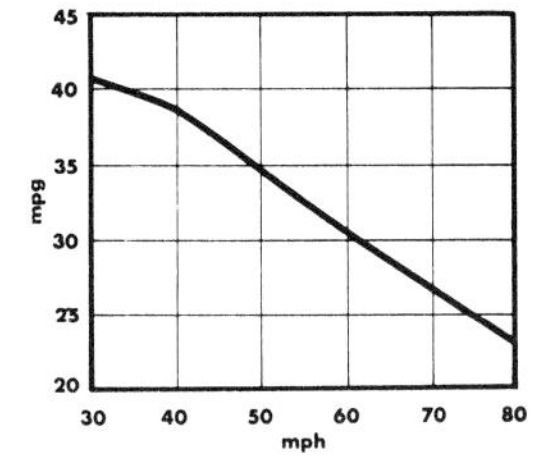

Tank capacity	14.5 galls
	65.9 litres
Max range	390 miles
	627 km
Test distance	1440 miles
	2317 km

*An estimated fuel consumption computed from the theoretical consumption at a steady speed midway between 30 mph and the car's maximum, less a 5 per cent allowance for acceleration.

NOISE

	dBA	Motor rating*
30 mph	62	9
50 mph	64	10
70 mph	71	17
Maximum†	77	26

*A rating where 1 = 30 dBA and 100 = 96 dBA, and where double the number means double the loudness.
†Peak noise level under full-throttle acceleration in 2nd.

SPEEDOMETER (mph)

Speedo	30	40	50	60	70	80	90
True mph	30	39	47	56	63	72	80

Distance recorder: 5.0 per cent fast

WEIGHT

	cwt	kg
Unladen weight*	25.5	1295
Weight as tested	29.2	1483

*with fuel for approx 50 miles.

Performance tests carried out by Motor's staff at the Motor Industry Research Association proving ground, Lindley.

Test Data: World Copyright reserved. No reproduction in whole or in part without written permission.

GENERAL SPECIFICATION

ENGINE

Cylinders	4 in-line
Capacity	1994 cc (121.6 cu in)
Bore/stroke	84.4/89.0mm
	(3.32/3.50in)
Cooling	Water
Block	Cast iron
Head	Light alloy
Valves	Sohc
Cam drive	Toothed belt
Compression	9.0:1
Carburetter	Twin SU HIF 44
Bearings	5 main
Max power	101 bhp (DIN) at 5250 rpm
Max torque	120 lb ft (DIN) at 3250 rpm

TRANSMISSION

Type	5-speed manual
Clutch dia	8.5in
Actuation	Hydraulic

Internal ratios and mph/1000 rpm

Top	0.792:1/23.2
4th	1.000:1/18.4
3rd	1.396:1/13.2
2nd	2.087:1/8.8
1st	3.320:1/5.5
Rev	3.428:1
Final drive	3.90:1

BODY/CHASSIS

Construction	Unitary
Protection	Seven stage phosphate pre-treatment for body-shell; cathodic electro-prime; PVC underbody seal; wax injection to box members and inside panels

SUSPENSION

Front	Ind. by MacPherson struts, coil springs, anti-roll bar.
Rear	Live axle located by torque tube, Watts linkage, radius arms, coil springs, telescopic dampers.

STEERING

Type	Rack and pinion
Assistance	Yes

BRAKES

Front	10.5in discs
Rear	9.0in drums
Park	On rear
Servo	Yes
Circuit	Split front/rear
Rear valve	Yes
Adjustment	Automatic

WHEELS/TYRES

Type	Pressed steel, 5.5J × 14
Tyres	175 HR 14
Pressures	28/30 psi F/R (normal)
	30/32 psi F/R (full load/high speed)

ELECTRICAL

Battery	12V, 66 Ah
Earth	Negative
Generator	Alternator, 65A
Fuses	18
Headlights	
type	Halogen
dip	110 W total
main	230 W total

Make: Rover
Model: 2000
Maker: Austin-Rover, International House, Bickenhill Lane, Birmingham B37 7HH. Tel: 021-779 6525.
Price: £5,980.00 plus £498.33 Car Tax and £971.75 VAT equals £7,450.08 total.

TheRivals

Other rivals include the Citroën CX Athena (£7,634). the Renault 20 TS (£7,845), the VW Passat GL5 S (£7,387), Alfa Romeo's Alfetta 2.0 (£7,250) and the Lancia Gamma (£8,195)

ROVER 2000 £7,450

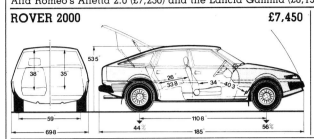

Power, bhp/rpm	101/5250
Torque, lb ft/rpm	120/3250
Tyres	175/ HR 14
Weight, cwt	25.5
Max speed, mph	102.5
0-60 mph, sec	12.4
30-50 mph in 4th, sec	11.3
Overall mpg	23.3
Touring mpg	26.9
Fuel grade, stars	4
Boot capacity, cu ft	12.7
Test Date	April 3, 1982

BL's SD1 range has been extended down-market with the new 4-cylinder Rover 2000. It shares the improved rearward visibility and instrumentation of all the '82 Rovers, but accommodation remains medicore in its class. Performance and economy reasonable for a large 2-litre, mediocre for the price, and low overall noise levels are marred by the quality of the engine note. Handling is responsive and safe, ride comfort better at speed than around town. Interior plush and comfortable.

AUSTIN AMBASSADOR 2.0 VANDEN PLAS £7,765

Power, bhp/rpm	100/5250
Torque, lb ft/rpm	120/3250
Tyres	185/70 HR 14
Weight, cwt	23.5
Max speed, mph	102.6
0-60 mph, sec	11.8
30-50 mph in 4th, sec	11.9
Overall mpg	23.6
Touring mpg	26.9
Fuel grade, stars	4
Boot capacity, cu ft	13.6
Test Date	April 3, 1982

Comfort is the keynote of BL's new Princess-derived five-door hatchback, especially in flagship Vandan Plas form which is plushly finished and lavishly equipped. Excellent ride, sumptuous seating, efficient heating/ventilation, lots of space and moderate noise levels are its main virtues. Performance and handling are adequate but not sporting, economy fair. Hatchback versatility has not compromised good boot space. Notchy gearchange and lack of fifth gear is its only weakness.

FORD GRANADA 2.3 L £7,999

Power, bhp/rpm	114/5300
Torque, lb ft/rpm	130/3000
Tyres	175 HR 14
Weight, cwt	26.1
Max speed, mph	105.2
0-60 mph, sec	11.4
30-50 mph in 4th, sec	10.4
Overall mpg	21.0
Touring mpg	27.4
Fuel grade, stars	4
Boot capacity, cu ft	13.2
Test Date	September 19, 1981

We haven't yet tested the £7,210 2-litre Granada in its 1982 form, but the 2.3-litre version is exceptionally refined, has an excellent ride, good handling and, as ever, generous accommodation. Other virtues include good build quality and tasteful interior trim, a pleasant gear-change and clear instrumentation. Performance and economy are nothing special though, and, despite a good level of standard equipment, it is rather expensive compared with most of its rivals.

OPEL REKORD 2.0S BERLINA £7,484

Power, bhp/rpm	100/5200
Torque, lb ft/rpm	116.5/3600
Tyres	185/70 SR 14
Weight, cwt	22.1
Max speed, mph	105.2
0-60 mph, sec	11.2
30-50 mph in 4th, sec	10.6
Overall mpg	22.3
Touring mpg	28.2
Fuel grade, stars	4
Boot capacity, cu ft	12.4
Test Date	February 4, 1978

In Berlina form, Opel's big 2-litre saloon provides an up-market alternative to the mechanically identical £7,031 Vauxhall Carlton (though the CD version is plusher still). Ride, roadholding and handling of a high standard, but unassisted steering heavy at low speed. Performance and economy average, pleasant gear-change. Roomy and comfortable with a large boot. Excellent finish, quite well equipped.

TALBOT TAGORA GL 5-SPEED £7,739

Power, bhp/rpm	113/5400
Torque, lb ft/rpm	133/3200
Tyres	175 SR 14
Weight, cwt	25.0
Max speed, mph	102.8
0-60 mph, sec	11.4
30-50 mph in 4th, sec	9.8
Overall mpg	24.3
Touring mpg	28.0
Fuel grade, stars	4
Boot capacity, cu ft	15.1
Test Date	May 16, 1981

Five-speed 2.2-litre four-cylinder version of Talbot's flagship, the Tagora GL isn't the quickest car in its class but it is the most economical. Other virtues include an exceptionally roomy and comfortable interior, a fine handling/ride compromise, a quick, easy gearchange and good refinement. The lack of an independent ventilation system, however, is a serious flaw and the interior could be more appealing.

VOLVO 244 DL O/D £7,359

Power, bhp/rpm	107/5500
Torque, lb ft/rpm	125/2500
Tyres	175 SR 14
Weight, cwt	25.2
Max speed, mph	100.1
0-60 mph, sec	12.7
30-50 mph in 4th, sec	9.9
Overall mpg	22.1
Touring mpg	26.6
Fuel grade, stars	4
Boot capacity, cu ft	13.1
Test Date	January 3, 1981

Most notable improvements for the latest 244 DL (tested in non-overdrive form) are a restyled front end and a new facia. Despite an increase in power output since the last 244 DL test, performance and economy remain just competitive for the class in which it must compete. Handling is still slightly ponderous but good comfort and refinement (up to 70 mph) make the Volvo an excellent long-distance tourer. Strong points are its quality, solidity, and built-in safety.

RoadTest

ALTHOUGH DIESEL car sales still account for only a miniscule portion of the UK car market, they have steadily grown over the last few years. If this continues then the 0.63 percentage of total sales that diesels took in 1981 is likely to increase to four per cent by 1985. Refreshingly, Austin Rover look well prepared to take advantage of this trend, and perhaps even give diesel car sales a significant boost by providing the habitually patriotic fleet car buyers with a home-based diesel.

At the moment Austin Rover only have the Rover 2400SD Turbo to satisfy the fleet operators' demand for the superior fuel efficiency provided by diesel engines. Other diesels are known to be under development, however, and it is to be hoped that an Austin Diesel will be forthcoming to set against that other recently introduced home-built diesel — the Vauxhall Cavalier 1.6 LD.

For the Rover it was decided that the relatively low volumes involved made it economically expedient to buy in a proprietary engine, a suitable in-house unit not being available. The engine chosen was a turbocharged, 2,393cc, four-cylinder unit built by the Italian VM concern — already used in larger-capacity form in the Alfetta Turbo-diesel. It has a cast iron block with wet cast iron cylinder liners and, unusually, there are separate aluminium cylinder heads for each cylinder. The overhead valves are pushrod operated.

The engine is of the indirect injection type (as are all current car diesel engines), with a pre-combustion chamber set into each cylinder head. Fuel injection is provided by a Bosch mechanical system and the inlet air is pressurised by a KKK turbocharger. Standard fitments for the Rover SD Turbo are an oil cooler, twin cooling fans and two heavy-duty 12V batteries. There are also revised engine and gearbox mounts, including hydraulically-damped front engine mounts, to absorb the low frequency vibrations of the diesel engine.

To suit the relatively narrow useable power band of the VM diesel the SD Turbo is fitted with the 3.9:1 final drive ratio of the Rover 2000. The internal ratios of the five-speed gearbox remain unchanged apart from top (from 0.792:1 to 0.77:1) which gives a relaxed 24 mph/1,000 rpm.

In other respects the SD Turbo is similar in specification to the Rover 2600S, with just slightly stiffer front

ROVER 2400SD TURBO

Intended to appeal mainly to the fleet car buyer, the diesel Rover is a desirable car in its own right

OOB 352X

springs being necessary to compensate for the additional weight of the diesel power unit. And, of course, it features the recent revisions and improvements made to the Rover range back in January which included a new, deeper rear window, a new front spoiler and a revised interior with a new instrument binnacle.

At £10,500 the Rover 2400SD Turbo falls midway between the 2600S (£9,975) and the 2600SE (£10,790), usefully supplementing a range which has only recently been extended downwards by the Rover 2000 and at the upper end by the sporty Rover Vitesse.

favourable testing conditions, we recorded a fastest lap around MIRA's banked circuit of 102.9 mph (best quarter mile, 103.4 mph) and a time of 14.2 sec for the sprint to 60 mph.

Among the SD Turbo's rivals we have listed for comparison only the Audi 80 Turbo diesel has a better 0-60 mph time (12.7 sec), while none of them can match the Rover's top speed. Even the petrol-engined Rover 2000 (102.5 mph) can't beat the diesel's maximum speed, though it has a better 0-60 mph time of 12.4 sec. In fact, when accelerating in fourth and fifth gears the SD Turbo is usefully its long-striding fifth gear.

In more give and take driving conditions, the superbly slick-changing five-speed gearbox, combined with a smooth clutch, means that it is no problem keeping the engine on boost and the lower four ratios are usefully closely packed to give maxima of 25, 40, 59 and 83 mph at 4,500 rpm. Starting the engine from cold is fairly prompt, as long as a few seconds are allowed after switch-on to allow the glow plug warning light to go out, but it is accompanied by a good deal of clattery diesel din and a not inconsiderable amount of smoke out of the exhaust.

Our testers found the Rover SD Turbo's power steering more to their liking than on other Rovers recently driven by *Motor*, being pleasantly direct and accurate, if still too light to transmit much feel. Other aspects of the Rover's handling remain excellent with its good roadholding being backed up by remarkable composure, for a live-axled car, over bumpy surfaces; and there is no adverse reaction to lifting off the throttle, or even hard braking, in mid corner.

Understeer, though, is much more predominant than in earlier versions of the Rover and there is now noticeable body roll, particularly in tighter corners taken quickly.

These rather softer handling characteristics have had a beneficial trade-off in terms of ride comfort, however. The Rover is still slightly jiggly over small bumps at low speeds and there is a tendency for the rear axle to thump over severe irregularities but, overall, the suspension copes well with a wide variety of road surfaces, being especially composed and comfortable at motorway speeds. The brakes performed admirably, providing powerful but progressive stopping power and having a good, solid pedal action.

Accommodation has never been one of the better features of the Rover, with combined front and rear legroom which is only mediocre by the standards of the executive car class. Legroom and headroom (further restricted by the standard sunroof) are barely

Left: comfortable, well-proportioned front seats have adjustable lumbar supports. Above: rear seat legroom is only mediocre by class standards

The most obvious rivals for the Rover in the executive diesel car market are the Audi 100 GL diesel (£9,318), Citroën CX 25D (£9,116), Mercedes 300D (£11,400) and Peugeot 604 SRD Turbo (£11,026). From within its own ranks perhaps the most interesting spark-ignition comparison is provided by the Rover 2000 which has similar performance but is almost £3,000 cheaper, at £7,750. It is also less plushly trimmed, though, and not as economical as the SD Turbo. Less expensive diesel-engined alternatives to the Rover include the new Audi 80 Turbo diesel (£7,616), Ford Granada 2.5 D (£7,716) Vauxhall Carlton 2.3D (£7,056), and Renault 20 GTD (£8,200).

On a 21:1 compression ratio the VM diesel engine produces 90 bhp (DIN) at 4,200 rpm and 142 lb ft (DIN) of torque at 2,350 rpm. Austin Rover claim that the SD Turbo is the fastest production diesel car on the UK market, quoting a top speed of 102 mph and a 0-60 mph acceleration time of 14.9 sec. If anything these claims are on the conservative side since, in not particularly

quicker than the 2000, with 30-50 mph in fourth taking 8.0 sec (11.3 sec for the 2000) and 50-70 mph in fifth being covered in 14.6 sec (2000, 20.2 sec).

A closer study of the SD Turbo's acceleration times in fifth gear clearly illustrates the characteristics of the turbo diesel engine. The 20-40 and 30-50 mph increments take 18.2 and 13.9 sec, respectively, and it is only when the 40-60 mph increment is reached that the fastest time is recorded — 12.4 sec. On the road this translates into an engine which is disappointingly lacking in response below about 2,000 rpm (it feels particularly sluggish when pulling away from rest) but once the turbocharger starts working effectively, the engine revs eagerly through the gears — albeit with a noticeable diesel clatter — to its 4,500 rpm red line. Cruising at speed is really the SD Turbo's forté; up to about 90mph in top the diesel quality of the engine is much less pronounced, and since the engine is always operating in its useable power band reasonable acceleration is available even with the gearbox left in

Warm up is quick, though, and fuss-free.

The SD Turbo's good level of overall performance is all the more commendable when it is considered that at 28.3 cwt it is almost 3 cwt heavier than the Rover 2000. Equally impressive, therefore, is that the diesel Rover also fulfils its economy brief, recording an overall fuel consumption figure of 29.6 mpg - as ever the result of hard driving — which is a full 25 per cent better than the Rover 2000. Compared with rival diesels the Rover has above average economy with just the (slower) Citroën CX 25D and the (lighter and smaller) Audi 80 Turbo diesel recording better overall consumption figures among those listed. In more gentle driving conditions, and around town, the Rover diesel is likely to be even more economical, relatively, than its petrol-engined counterparts and most owners should find 35 mpg within their grasp, at which rate of consumption each 14.5 gallon tankful of diesel fuel would give an excellent range of more than 500 miles.

adequate for tall drivers and with the front seats fully back, space in the rear is restricted. The boot is generously sized, though, and the Rover offers superior versatility compared with most of its rivals thanks to the large hatchback and folding rear seats. Interior stowage for minor oddments is well provided for by shin bins, a facia top shelf, and a cassette holder between the front seats.

Although tall drivers will find legroom rather restricted (our 6ft 4in tester also noted that the top sector of the instruments was shrouded, for him, by the top of the binnacle) the driving position is generally comfortable, helped by an adjustable — if over-large for some tastes — steering wheel and good pedal layout. The standard Austin Rover column stalk set up works well enough and most of the minor switchgear is within easy reach but the push-push switches located in the instrument binnacle take some learning. Generously proportioned and well-shaped seats provide good support and comfort over long distances with an adjust-

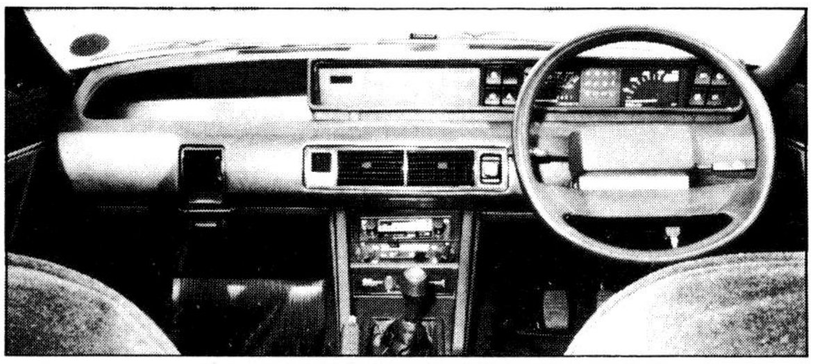

Above: attractive '82 Rover facia. Left: messily calibrated speedometer

able lumbar support helping to cope with the differing requirements of variously-sized occupants.

Visibility has been much improved by the larger tailgate window but it is still difficult to judge the extremities of the car when parking. On the move, good mirrors, effective headlights, and efficient front and rear wash/wipe systems all help to ensure good all-round visibility. The new Rover instrument layout is attractive and comprehensive, marred only by the densely-packed markings on the speedometer and the minor gauges being slightly out of the driver's line of sight.

The Rover's heating and ventilation systems are well suited to the vagaries of the British climate, the heater providing a powerful but finely controllable output while the separate fan-boostable fresh air vents in the centre of the facia allow for the desirable combination of cool air for the face and warm air for the footwells. A minor backward step noted by one of our testers, though, is that the ideally-located vent that was previously positioned directly in front of the driver, has disappeared in the new facia layout.

As already mentioned, the SD Turbo rarely lets you forget that it is diesel-powered with an insistent clatter occurring on start-up and when pressed hard through the gears. There is also a noticeable whistle from the turbocharger as the engine comes on boost at around 2,000 rpm. Overall, though, the Rover is respectably refined, as befits its executive car image; to some extent it is the low levels of wind and road noise that tend to highlight the engine noise, which in fact, is never excessively intrusive. At motorway speeds in fifth gear it is sufficiently well suppressed to allow pleasantly relaxed cruising.

Inside, the Rover diesel also fulfils its top-car image with a tasteful combination of colours and materials, including very attractive pin-striped velour trim for the seats and walnut veneer insets on the door trims. This luxurious and well-assembled feel is followed through to the exterior which features acceptably snug panel fits and a truly lustrous paint finish.

The level of equipment is generally as would be expected on a car costing £10,500 with standard items including the sliding steel sunroof, central locking for the doors and the hatchback, electric window lifters front and rear, adjustable lumbar support on the front seats, and a digital clock cum stop watch. The stereo radio/cassette fitted to our test car is, disappointingly, an optional extra, the standard fitting being a push button MW/LW radio.

Austin Rover's first diesel car for nearly twenty years lives up to its makers' "fastest diesel" claims and also delivers the goods as far as fuel economy is concerned. The Rover 2400SD Turbo retains all the better attributes of the capable Rover range and while the driver is unlikely to forget he is sitting behind a diesel engine he can take comfort from the car's parsimonious thirst for fuel and the plushness of his surroundings. The diesel Rover will undoubtedly appeal to fleet operators looking for more economical cars for their executives; and the private owner who wants an economy luxury car, and isn't too bothered about performance, should also find the Rover a very attractive proposition.

Plenty of room under the Rover's bonnet for the VM turbocharged diesel engine. Note the twin 12V batteries in the front of the compartment

MOTOR ROAD TEST No 54/82 ●

ROVER 2400 SD TURBO

PERFORMANCE

WEATHER CONDITIONS

Wind	20 mph
Temperature	53°F/15°C
Barometer	988 mbar
Surface	Dry tarmacadam

MAXIMUM SPEEDS

	mph	kph
Banked circuit	102.9	165.6
Best ¼ mile	103.4	166.4
Terminal Speeds:		
at ¼ mile	67	108
at kilometre	85	137
at mile	93	150
Speeds in gears (at 4,500 rpm):		
1st	25	40
2nd	40	64
3rd	59	95
4th	83	134

ACCELERATION FROM REST

mph	sec	kph	sec
0-30	4.6	0-40	3.4
0-40	6.9	0-60	6.3
0-50	10.3	0-80	10.3
0-60	14.2	0-100	15.8
0-70	21.4	0-120	25.0
0-80	29.5	0-140	41.3
0-90	46.4		
Stand'g ¼	19.6	Stand'g km	36.7

ACCELERATION IN TOP

mph	sec	kph	sec
20-40	18.2	40-60	10.9
30-50	13.9	60-80	8.4
40-60	12.4	80-100	7.9
50-70	14.6	100-120	11.2
60-80	18.3		

ACCELERATION IN 4TH

mph	sec	kph	sec
20-40	10.8	40-60	6.5
30-50	8.0	60-80	4.8
40-60	8.2	80-100	6.2
50-70	12.0	100-120	9.7
60-80	16.0		

FUEL CONSUMPTION

Touring*	See text
Overall	29.6 mpg 9.5 litres/100 km
Govt tests (not obligatory)	30.2 mpg (urban) 46.7 mpg (56 mph) 32.7 mpg (75 mph)
Fuel grade	Diesel
Tank capacity	14.5 galls 66 litres
Max range*	507 miles 816 km
Test distance	1,210 miles 1,947 km

*Based on an estimated touring consumption of 35 mpg

NOISE

	dBA	Motor rating*
30 mph	63	9.5
50 mph	66	12
70 mph	73	19
Maximum†	78	28

*A rating where 1=30 dBA, and 100=96 dBA, and where double the number means double the loudness

†Peak noise level under full-throttle acceleration in 2nd.

SPEEDOMETER (mph)

Speedo	30	40	50	60	70	80	90
True mph	29	38	46	55	64	73	83

Distance recorder: 0.4 per cent slow

WEIGHT

	cwt	kg
Unladen weight*	28.3	1438
Weight as tested	32.0	1626

*with fuel for approx 50 miles

Performance tests carried out by Motor's staff at the Motor Industry Research Association proving ground, Lindley.

Test Data: World Copyright reserved. No reproduction in whole or part without written permission.

GENERAL SPECIFICATION

ENGINE

Cylinders	4 in-line
Capacity	2,393cc (146.0 cu in)
Bore/stroke	92/90mm (3.62/3.54in)
Cooling	Water
Block	Cast iron
Heads	Aluminium alloy
Valves	Pushrod ohv
Cam drive	Gear
Compression	21:1
Fuel system	Bosch mechanical fuel injection, KKK turbocharger
Bearings	5 main
Max power	90 bhp (DIN) at 4,200 rpm
Max torque	142 lb ft (DIN) at 2,350 rpm

TRANSMISSION

Type	5-speed, manual
Clutch dia	9.5in
Actuation	Hydraulic
Internal ratios	and mph/1,000 rpm
Top	0.77:1/24.0
4th	1.00:1/18.5
3rd	1.396:1/13.2
2nd	2.087:1/8.9
1st	3.321:1/5.6
Rev	3.428:1
Final drive	3.9:1

BODY/CHASSIS

Construction	Unitary, all steel
Protection	Seven stage phosphate pre-treatment for bodyshell; cathodic primer application; pvc underbody seal; wax injection of hollow body sections

SUSPENSION

Front	Independent by MacPherson struts; coil springs; anti-roll bar
Rear	Live axle located by torque tube, Watts linkage and radius arms; coil springs, self-levelling dampers

STEERING

Type	Rack and pinion
Assistance	Yes

BRAKES

Front	Discs,10.2in dia.
Rear	Drums, 9.0in dia
Park	On rear
Servo	Yes
Circuit	Dual, split front/rear
Rear valve	Yes
Adjustment	Automatic

WHEELS/TYRES

Type	Pressed steel, 5½J × 14
Tyres	175 HR 14
Pressures	28/30 psi F/R (normal) 30/32 psi F/R (full load)

ELECTRICAL

Battery	2 × 12V, 55Ah
Earth	Negative
Generator	Alternator, 65A
Fuses	18
Headlights	
type	Halogen
dip	110 W total
main	230 W total

Make: Rover. **Model**: 2400 SD Turbo.
Maker: Austin Rover Group Ltd, Canley Road, Canley, Coventry CV5 6QX. Tel: 0203 70111
Price: £8,428.00 plus £702.33 Car Tax and £1,369.55 VAT equals £10,499.88 total. Optional extra on test car: Stereo radio/cassette, £169.02. Price as tested, £10,668.90.

TheRivals

Other rivals include the Audi 100 GL diesel (£9,318), Ford Granada 2.5D (£7,716), Vauxhall Carlton 2.3D (£7,056) and Renault 20 GTD (£8,200).

ROVER 2400SD TURBO £10,500

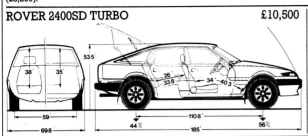

Power, bhp/rpm	90/4200
Torque, lb ft/rpm	142/2350
Tyres	175 HR 14
Weight, cwt	28.3
Max speed, mph	102.9
0-60 mph, sec	14.2
30-50 mph in 4th, sec	8.0
Overall mpg	29.6
Touring mpg	—
Fuel grade, stars	Diesel
Boot capacity, cu ft	12.7
Test Date	October 30, 1982

Austin Rover's up-market diesel Rover has excellent performance, for a diesel, and good fuel economy. Turbocharged four-cylinder engine is intrusive when pressed hard but overall refinement is good. Other Rover attributes remain intact including capable handling, a comfortable ride, powerful brakes, a slick-changing five-speed gearbox, luxurious interior trim, and a very effective heating and ventilation system. Accommodation is only mediocre for the class, though.

AUDI 80 TURBO DIESEL £7,616

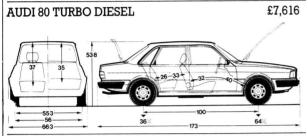

Power, bhp/rpm	70/4500
Torque, lb ft/rpm	98/2600
Tyres	165 SR 13
Weight, cwt	19.3
Max speed, mph	97.2
0-60 mph, sec	12.7
30-50 mph in 4th, sec	9.6
Overall mpg	37.4
Touring mpg	—
Fuel grade, stars	Diesel
Boot capacity, cu ft	11.0
Test Date	Not published

Remarkably quick considering its relatively small capacity diesel engine, and exceptionally economical, the Audi 80 turbo diesel makes a strong case for the diesel car. Good roadholding and vice-free handling is combined with a comfortable, if firmish, ride. Really competes in the next class down from the Rover but for its size, and price, it features a reasonably roomy well-trimmed interior and a competitive level of standard equipment. Heating and ventilation are powerful and effective.

CITROEN CX 25D £9,116

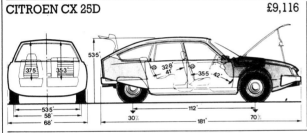

Power, bhp/rpm	75/4250
Torque, lb ft/rpm	111/2000
Tyres	185 SR 14 (front) 175 SR 14 (rear)
Weight, cwt	26.6
Max speed, mph	96.3
0-60 mph, sec	16.0
30-50 mph in 4th, sec	8.9
Overall mpg	33.4
Touring mpg	—
Fuel grade, stars	Diesel
Boot capacity, cu ft	10.2
Test Date	August 23, 1980

Renamed for the 1983 model year, Citroën's diesel version of the CX remains one of the quickest and most economical big diesels tested by *Motor*. It is also very refined and well appointed and equipped. Other CX virtues, such as the comfortable ride, spacious interior and relaxed high-speed cruising, are unaltered but we remained unimpressed by the poor instrumentation, unpleasant power steering and the over-sensitive fully-powered hydraulic braking system.

MERCEDES 300D £11,400

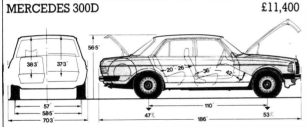

Power, bhp/rpm	88/4400
Torque, lb ft/rpm	127/2400
Tyres	175 SR 14
Weight, cwt	28.7
Max speed, mph	88.4
0-60 mph, sec	18.5
30-50 mph in k'down, sec	7.8
Overall mpg	24.2
Touring mpg	—
Fuel grade, stars	Diesel
Boot capacity, cu ft	14.2
Test Date	August 18, 1979

Five-cylinder, diesel-engined Mercedes is more economical than petrol-engined equivalents but has a substantial performance deficit (power has been increased since our test, though) only partly compensated by good refinement and smooth automatic transmission. Like its stablemates, a sure-footed car with excellent brakes, roomy interior, good heating and ventilation, but mediocre ride comfort. Expensive but very well finished.

PEUGEOT 604 SRD TURBO £11,026

Power, bhp/rpm	80/4150
Torque, lb ft/rpm	130/2000
Tyres	175 HR 14
Weight, cwt	29.2
Max speed, mph	94.9
0-60 mph, sec	16.6
30-50 mph in 4th, sec	10.4
Overall mpg	26.4
Touring mpg	—
Fuel grade, stars	Diesel
Boot capacity, cu ft	12.6
Test Date	February 18, 1980

Europe's first turbocharged diesel car is still a strong contender in the prestige diesel market. Reasonable performance and refinement, by diesel standards, from "blown" version of Peugeot's 2.3-litre four-cylinder diesel but the Rover is faster and more economical. Usual 604 attributes of excellent accommodation, steering, handling and ride spoiled only by poor driving position and complicated heating system.

ROVER 2000 £7,750

Power, bhp/rpm	101/5250
Torque, lb ft/rpm	120/3250
Tyres	175 HR 14
Weight, cwt	25.5
Max speed, mph	102.5
0-60 mph, sec	12.4
30-50 mph in 4th, sec	11.3
Overall mpg	23.3
Touring mpg	26.9
Fuel grade, stars	4
Boot capacity, cu ft	12.7
Test Date	April 3, 1982

Austin Rover have extended the SD1 range down market with the four-cylinder Rover 2000. Modifications on the '82 Rovers have improved rearward visibility and instrumentation but accommodation is only mediocre for the class. Performance is slightly down compared to the Rover diesel, and economy significantly so, but it is competitive with other large-bodied 2-litre petrol-engined cars. Reasonably refined and has responsive and safe handling combined with good ride comfort.

Auto TEST Rover Vitesse

Fast and efficient

Rover Vitesse
Rover Vitesse performance version of SD1 launched in December 1982. Lucas L fuel injection, 9.75-to-1 compression ratio, plus better inlet and exhaust breathing permits 190 bhp (DIN) at 5,280 rpm and 220 lb. ft. torque at 4,000 rpm. Car also features four pot front calipers, plus lower and 20 per cent stiffer suspension. Aerodynamic changes include large tail gate spoiler and rear wheel arch fairings. C_d figure is a respectable 0.36.

PRODUCED AND SOLD BY:
Austin Rover Group Ltd.,
Canley Road,
Canley,
Coventry CV5 6QX

IT SEEMS that no matter what constraints are put on the motoring public, there will always be a market for high performance cars, either in the guise of an out-and-out sports machine or, like the Rover Vitesse, intended as a high performance variant of an existing range, capitalizing on the recent success earned by racing versions of the car.

Certainly it has been clear ever since the car was introduced (in October 1977) that significant increases in power and torque would be possible without any sacrifice in refinement. Main mechanical change on Rover's rugged all-aluminium pushrod ohv 3,528 c.c. V8 is the adoption of Lucas L electronic fuel injection (used for some time in other markets to meet stringent exhaust emission regulations). Reprofiled inlet ports improve gas flow, and the compression ratio is upped from 9.25 to 9.75-to-1. These modifications account for outputs rising from the normal ʹ0SE's 155 bhp (DIN) at 5,250 ʹ,ʋ,n, and 198lb.ft. torque at 2,500rpm, to 190bhp (DIN) at 5,280rpm and a hefty 220 lb.ft. torque peaking much higher up at 4,000 rpm.

Transmission modifications are limited to shot peening the gears to increase their fatigue resistance, and stronger gearbox bearings. In place of the standard wheel and tyre fitment, the Vitesse runs on 6½in. wide, 15in. diameter cast alloy rims fitted with 205/60VR ultra low profile tyres. On a 3.08-to-1 final drive and 0.79-to-1 fifth gear, overall gearing is 29.4 mph per 1,000 rpm, ie, slightly higher overdrive gearing than is found in the normal Rover V8.

Spring rates have been increased by around 20 per cent and the body sits an inch lower. For a car in this class Rover felt ʹt 2600/3500 Nivomat rear ʹ.ʹelling units should be retained and on the Vitesse these (suitably re-calibrated) are used in conjunction with variable rate springs. This is also the first production application of the hitherto special four-pot brake caliper and ventilated disc first seen in competition, and then on the police specification Rovers. MacPherson struts are used in front. The beam rear axle is located via a torque tube, trailing arms and a Watt linkage as normal, but a welcome modification has been a reduction in steering rack ratio to give 3.0 instead of 2.75 turns from lock to lock, and the system is now arranged to reduce the servo effect at speed.

All Vitesses have two-tone grey cloth upholstery, polished wood dash and door cappings. Outside they are clearly distinguished by multi-spoke alloy wheels and very large rear spoiler which according to factory claims not only adds a significant degree of down force at speed, but is also largely responsible for the drag coefficient dropping from the 3500SE's C_d of 0.39 to 0.36

Multi spoke alloy wheels, a large rear deck spoiler, and Vitesse badging (on the rear and sides) distinguish the Vitesse from outside. Front air dam (common to other models) houses fog lamps. Overriders contain headlamp washer jets

The Vitesse tipped MIRA's scales at 28.0 cwt (against 28.3 cwt for the SE) distributed 56/44 front to rear.

Performance
Flexibly potent

For some time it has been clear that with only a little attention, the 3.5-litre Rover V8 could be persuaded to release its potential without any real sacrifice in its flexibility.

Although we could not induce this particular example to match factory performance claims (135 mph and 0-60 mph in 7.1sec), this large hatchback car easily equalled or bettered the performance provided by other high performance cars in the class. During standing start acceleration runs with any SD1 Rover, one always notes the lack of attitude change as the clutch is engaged (guaranteed by the anti-squat characteristics of a torque tube axle location), but with so much torque, no limited slip differential, and possibly a wrong-side torque tube pivot, wheelspin is easy to provoke.

Various techniques were tried in getting the car off the line; the most effective proved to be dropping the clutch with approximately 4,000 rpm indicated and letting rather frantic wheelspin blend into forward momentum. It takes a very fast car indeed to better the Vitesse's 0 to 30, 60 and 100 mph in 2.7, 7.6 and 20.7 sec. We went on to record 120 mph in 35.5 sec (close to the 34.2 recorded by the latest 139 mph BMW 635CSi Coupé), and all within the confines of MIRA's one-mile horizontal straights.

The red sector on the rev counter (100 rpm optimistic on test car) starts at 5,500 rpm. At that limit maxima in the lower gears are 38, 61, 92 and 128 mph. Fifth gear provides a significant overdrive effect — very relaxed motorway cruising — but falls some way short of being the ideal ratio for the car to achieve its maximum speed. The Vitesse slowly worked its way up to a mean maximum of 130 mph, with a best with-wind speed of 133 mph. Even at the latter speed the engine is only revving at 4,500

rpm or nearly 800 rpm below the peak power point. On the other hand, it would be necessary to rev the engine 300 rpm into the red sector and 500 rpm over peak power to achieve the claimed 135 mph maximum in fourth.

The slightly disappointing maximum speed was balanced by the Vitesse's deliciously torquey mid-range "go" and excellent flexibility. The car pulls away without fuss from 10 mph in fourth and begins to pull strongly at 1,500 rpm. Investigation of the in-the-gear acceleration figures shows that for the considerable increase in performance at the top end and much freer revving nature the Vitesse engine has lost virtually nothing of the "standard" SD1's low end torque.

The result is a car that is equally at ease being trickled through the traffic, or being fully exploited when it becomes eager and effortlessly swift, eating up the road ahead, to the accompaniment of a delightfully purposeful growl on wide open throttle. Were it legally possible, the car's natural cruising gait would be around 100 mph when the engine is turning over at a mere 3,400 rpm.

As with all present day fuel injection systems cold start enrichment is automatic. The Lucas "L" system offered immediate cold start characteristics. There were no hesitations or flat spots to mar driveability during a commendably short warm-up period, but we did notice a minor hesitancy in power delivery around 2,500 rpm when the engine was warm.

Economy
Excellent

As if to emphasize the fact that when higher compression ratios are used with the current breed of fuel injection systems (and low aerodynamic drag), performance need not necessarily be at the expense of fuel economy, the Vitesse returned 21.8 mpg — the best overall fuel consumption figure we have seen for an SD1 V8 on road test. Its worst interim figure was 20.3 mpg which included performance testing and several trips across London, and we could imagine owners regu-

larly managing 23-25 mpg. It seems that Austin Rover have a car that is as least as economical as the obvious German competition — and more so if the overall performance is taken into account. In spite of this improvement in efficiency the range could still be improved. The tank holds 14.5 gallons and it is unlikely that one will be able to cover more than 250 miles before the fuel warning light starts to blink. The absolute range is an unexceptional 300 miles so those contemplating a long journey may feel it worthwhile to trickle fill the gallon or so it takes to give a true brim. Unfortunately this procedure takes several minutes, therefore is likely to inconvenience others, and gain very little if any time in the long run. The engine consumed a half-litre of oil during the 919 mile test period.

Noise
Wind and road

Once again we are bound to comment that in spite of the SD1's competitively wind cheating profile, wind noise intrusion is rather worse than average particularly for this class of car. It builds quite strongly from the legal limit onwards, and is the most obvious source of noise when travelling much above 80 mph.

Ultra-low profile tyres are apt to produce more noise than 70 or 80 series rubber, and the Vitesse does develop a noticeable — if by no means wearing — degree of tyre roar on coarse surfaces.

There is also the expected tyre-thump on potholes and drain covers and on the test car this excited a low frequency body boom. This "panting" was also noticed at constant speeds when running over uneven or patched surfaces. The Vitesse is an acceptably refined car at speed and, wind noise apart, not at all tiring on long hauls. Rover's V8 is smooth enough. It has a rather endearing uneven beat all of its own; at any cruising speed below 110 mph it is barely audible, and as we have mentioned, it produces a muffled but purposeful growl under hard acceleration that is entirely in character with the car. As in previous SD1 manual gearbox cars there is a lot of whine in third and, more particularly, second gears.

Aluminium V8 nestles snugly in SD1 engine bay. Lucas L fuel injection air metering unit is interposed between air cleaner cannister (front left) and inlet manifold plenum chamber

Road behaviour
Acceptable

With criticisms of previous SD1s' steering centring on sensitivity of response and lightness, the alteration in gearing to provide 3.0 instead of 2.75 turns (covering a very tight for the class 34ft turning circle) is a welcome one, however in the Vitesse's case the improved response resulting from the stiffer than standard suspension, and ultra-low profile Pirelli P6 tyres leave the car's initial response to the wheel feeling much as before. This quick gearing and the relatively low efforts needed to steer, make it a delightfully nimble car in town and to manoeuvre in and out of tight spaces. However, one notices little of the assistance reduction that is supposed to occur at speed, and we feel no harm could result from more weighting — or less assistance — particularly when trying to place the car accurately in fast bends. In

contrast, the gearchange is disappointingly stiff and notchy and the clutch fairly heavy. Thus the controls have an oddly unharmonious feel about them.

The heavily rear spoilered Vitesse is pleasingly stable in a straight line, and unlike some recently tested Rover SD1s, it naturally resists the effects of blustery conditions, rather than having to be steered to correct.

The main disappointment (as on other SD1s) is the car's ride quality. On larger bumps taken at moderate speed it can be felt reaching the limits of suspension travel (then reacting upwards) though this is a tolerably cushioned movement as progressive rate polyurethane "spring aids" are used (rather than the rubber bump stops of other Rovers). Even on the surprisingly low recommended "normal driving" front and rear tyre pressures of 24/26lb the car notices minor

unevennessses in apparently flat road surfaces.

This ride "busy-ness" does diminish with speed. Indeed the more "work" that is put into the suspension the better the car becomes. It soaks up the average British B road commendably well with well controlled suspension movements and throughout the test period we did not encounter any of the rear axle hop one sometimes encounters in the Vitesse's more prosaic stablemates.

There is very little cornering roll and on dry roads the ultra-low profile tyres ensure that the Vitesse is able to generate a very satisfying level of cornering grip. In the wet, excess driving torque in the lower gears is usually harmlessly released via wheelspin before a tail slide develops.

Vitesse handling balance is something of a paradox. There is

the crisp initial response; at normal cornering speeds, the car goes immediately where it is pointed. Such a reaction gives the impression that the ultimate balance will be near neutral. In fact, as cornering speeds are built up it begins to understeer strongly, unless the throttle is closed, but even then it can rarely be provoked into a tail slide, and we were moved to wonder if the strong understeering balance has not been built into all SD1s to counter the potentially upsetting effects of coarse steering inputs.

The Vitesse must be one of the very few cars of such weight and performance that does not rely on disc brakes front and back, yet this does not prevent the car having adequate braking. The pedal has a reassuringly firm feel to it, and the response pattern follows a near linearly progressive pattern until peak deceleration are called for when there is a slight (and ideal) steepening of the effort curve, which will help inhibit locking brakes in panic. In the event the Vitesse achieved excellent 1.05g with a 120lb load (after 0.96g with 100lb), any further effort locking the front wheels and reducing the slowing rate to a meagre 0.8g. In spite of a gradual doubling of pedal efforts in the fade test (10 consecutive 0.5g stops from 90 mph) pedal loads did not become seriously high, and there was no increase in pedal travel that might have indicated the onset of fade, but some judder accompanied the later runs, and when braking hard from high speed, a certain vagueness beset the steering. With a mighty heave, the handbrake managed to hold the car on the 1 in 3 but considering it is operating on large drum brakes, the just-legal 0.26g it managed on the flat was disappointing.

Behind the wheel
Quartic? No thanks

Although the seats look much like those fitted in other models they are more contoured in the cushion and back, therefore offer rather better sideways location. There is only *just* enough rearward adjustment for a 6ft driver and with the manually operated sliding sunshine roof fitted, headroom is unusually limited for a car of this size, taller testers complaining that their heads came firmly into contact with the "cant rail", with any sideways movement.

Throttle and brake are well positioned for heel and toe operation. but all those who drove the car would have dearly liked Rover to be able to discard their "Quartic" steering wheel (presumably so shaped to get a better view of the instruments) in favour of a conventional three- or four-spoke sports type. It is adjustable for reach and rake (via a turnwheel reached by opening the driver's side glovebox) and

Instrument binnacle houses (from right to left) push button switches for foglamps, rear wipe and heated rear window, rev counter, speedometer, more switches for hazard warning, interior light, and one to isolate passengers' electric windows, then fuel contents, water temperature, oil pressure gauges, and trip computer readout. Behind the universally disliked "Quartic" steering wheel are stalk controls operating indicators/dip/ horn/headlamp flash on left and wipe/wash on right. Main lights switch (hidden) is on left of column. Centre console houses radio/cassette, heating and ventilation controls, and on-board computer keyboard.

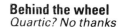

Good quality cloth upholstered front seats are comfortable but lack rearward adjustment. Note duct in facia to take heated air to door for side window demist Rear seat passengers are located in well contoured seats, reading lights are provided

taller drivers will find this move-￢ant particularly useful if they ⌐ to prevent the steering wheel rim masking the speedometer and rev counter.

The main dials have rather unusual quadrant shaped sweeps. To their right is a group of switches (some push button, others rocker) dealing with front and rear fog lights, interior light, rear wash/wipe, (intermittent or linked operation). The left hand set looks after rear window demist, rear window lift isolation, and hazard. Ancillary instruments; oil pressure, water temperature and fuel contents gauges are in the left hand section of the SD1's long instrument binnacle, together with the LED clock, which also serves as a display for the on-board computer.

Stalk controls are familiar Rover; a little springy in use with the left working the indicators/horn/dip/flash, and the right the ꓕꓕen wipe/wash, which in addition to the usual functions has a linked wipe/wash facility, and works the high pressure jet headlamp washers.

One of the inevitable results of the SD1's sloping down nose and high tail, is that the newcomer may find it an awkward car to judge widths in, or reverse (in spite of the larger rear window of the Mk 2 model). One adjusts by taking that little bit of extra care in tight situations, and by learning to make good use of the two excellent power operated door mirrors.

The heating and ventilation system is simple to understand and work. Sliders look after temperature, fan/fresh air/recirculating modes. Knobs deal with directional control and fresh air flow. The system produces a good quantity of accurately controllable warm and fresh air, and heated air is ducted through the doors to look after side window demist. Fresh air flow is quite independent of the heat control (unlike many present day systems) so there is always the option of cool air at face level no

matter what the heat setting chosen. Although there is not much ram flow available the fan operates reasonably on quietly its first speed and boosts flow considerably.

Living with the Vitesse

Attractive two-tone grey cloth trim is unique to the Vitesse, and to confirm this is a top-of-the-range Rover, there are wood cappings on the facia and doors. In addition to a high level of equipment, the Vitesse comes as standard with a Smiths on-board computer operating from a panel of buttons in the centre console. Though nothing like as comprehensive (or complex) as the device found in BMWs, it is far simpler to operate, and provides all the functions a driver could reasonably ask for; read-outs of instantaneous and average fuel consumption (both extremely accurate), trip distance, average speed, plus the usual timer functions.

Access to the rear seats is straightforward. The seats themselves are comfortable enough, but as the SD1's fastback shape implies, rear headroom – and to a lesser extent legroom – becomes a problem for those over 6ft in height. Of course the SD1's great strength is its hatch back and therefore unusual (for this class of car) load carrying versatility. Gas struts assist opening and prop the fifth door to reveal a space able to accep a good luggage load (there is further space for oddments under the rear floor in alongside the spare wheel). By releasing a single centre mounted catch, the rear seat back folds down to provide an enormous load space, the one minor drawback here being the high sill over which heavy items have to be lifted. The Vitesse retains the Nivomat rear damper cum levelling units, so load carrying does not affect the car's attitude

– a very useful feature particularly when driving at night.

Like other Rovers, the Vitesse also does pretty well for oddments space because although there are no door bins or pockets, there are the usual drop down gloveboxes on both the driver's and passenger's side, and the facia top is lipped to retain articles, also storage for tape cassettes is provided in a lidded centre console. Removing the rubber mat covering this area reveals a conveniently placed fuse box cover, but quite inexplicably, there are a further six fuses mounted behind the carpet covering on inner wheel arch.

The bonnet release is reached by opening the driver's side glovebox. The all-aluminium Rover V8 is topped by a purposeful

looking fuel injection inlet system, which does not prevent fluid level checks being made as simply as on other models.

The central door locking is a boon (the rear hatch has to be independetly unlocked using the same key as for the fuel filler cover and gloveboxes) and of the many other details we liked the rapidity with which the electric windows worked, and the provision of underbonnet and rear luggage compartment lighting. The Vitesse was fitted with a manually operated sliding sunshine roof (which unfortunately has no tipping mode) and a Phillips PLL self-seeking stereo radio cassette player and associated four speaker sound

system. This excited praise for its signal reception and reproduction of tapes.

Maintenance schedules call for attention at unusually infrequent 12,000 mile intervals.

The Rover range

The manual-only Vitesse costs £14,950 and is at the top of the SD1 range, which in reverse order consists of the Vanden Plas £13,900, 3500SE £12,250, 2600SE £10,790 (automatic is a no-cost option on the latter pair), 2600S £9,975, 2400 SD Diesel Turbo £10,500, 2300S £9,450, 2300 £8,290, and 2000 at £7,750. Automatic transmission on lower capacity petrol cars is £307 extra.

Under floor well is capable of housing quite bulky objects in addition to jack and tools Sturdy parcel shelf hinges with rear door, to reveal fully carpeted and generously proportioned luggage compartment Obvious wheel arch intrusion (and high rear sill) does not minimize the usefulness of Rover Vitesse load area

HOW THE ROVER VITESSE PERFORMS

TEST CONDITIONS:

Figures taken at 2,533 miles by our own staff at the Motor Industry Research Association proving ground at Nuneaton, and at the Vauxhall test track at Millbrook. All Autocar test results are subject to world copyright and may not be reproduced in whole or part without the Editor's written permission.

Wind: 10-18 mph
Temperature: 8 deg C (46 deg F)
Barometer: 29.2in. Hg (990 mbar)
Humidity: 100 per cent
Surface: dry asphalt and concrete
Test distance: 919 miles

MAXIMUM SPEEDS

Gear	mph	kph	rpm
OD Top (mean)	130	209	4,400
(best)	133	214	4,500
4th	128	206	5,500
3rd	92	148	5,500
2nd	61	98	5,500
1st	38	61	5,500

ACCELERATION

FROM REST

True mph	Time (sec)	Speedo mph
30	2.7	30
40	4.2	40
50	5.9	50
60	7.6	61
70	10.5	72
80	13.2	83
90	16.0	95
100	20.7	106
110	27.3	116
120	35.5	126
130	–	137

Standing ¼-mile: 15.9 sec, 90 mph
Standing km: 29.3 sec, 114 mph

IN EACH GEAR

mph	Top	4th	3rd	2nd
10-30		9.9	6.1	3.7
20-40	12.4	8.1	5.5	3.5
30-50	10.9	7.7	5.2	3.2
40-60	10.6	7.5	4.9	3.5
50-70	12.0	7.7	5.2	–
60-80	12.9	8.2	5.5	–
70-90	13.5	8.3	6.2	–
80-100	15.8	9.2	–	–
90-100	19.4	11.3	–	–
100-110	–	14.8	–	–

FUEL CONSUMPTION

Overall mpg:
21.8 (13.0 litres/100km)
4.8 mpl

Autocar constant speed fuel consumption measuring gear incompatible with fuel injection

Autocar formula:	Hard 19.6mpg
Driving and	Average 24.0mpg
conditions	Gentle 28.3mpg

Grade of fuel: Premium, 4-star (97 RM)
Fuel tank: 14.5 Imp. galls (66 litres)
Mileage recorder reads: 3.7 per cent long

Official fuel consumption figures
(ECE laboratory test conditions; not necessarily related to Autocar figures)
Urban cycle: 18.5 mpg
Steady 56 mph: 37.7 mpg
Steady 75 mph: 30.1 mpg

OIL CONSUMPTION

(SAE 15/50) 1,000 miles/pint

BRAKING

Fade *(from 90 mph in neutral)*
Pedal load for 0.5g stops in lb

	start/end		start/end
1	32/28	6	40/78
2	30/36	7	44/72
3	36/44	8	48/78
4	36/46	9	48/78
5	40/66	10	52/78

Response *(from 30 mph in neutral)*

Load	g	Distance
40 lb	0.46	65 ft
60 lb	0.70	43 ft
80 lb	0.89	34 ft
100 lb	0.96	31.3 ft
120 lb	1.05	115 ft
Handbrake	0.26	116 ft

Max. gradient: 1 in 3

CLUTCH Pedal 36 lb; Travel 5.3in.

WEIGHT

Kerb, 28.0 cwt/3,136 lb/1,424 kg
(Distribution F/R, 56/44)
Test, 31.3 cwt/3,508 lb/1,593 kg
Max. payload, 1,049 lb/476 kg

DIMENSIONS

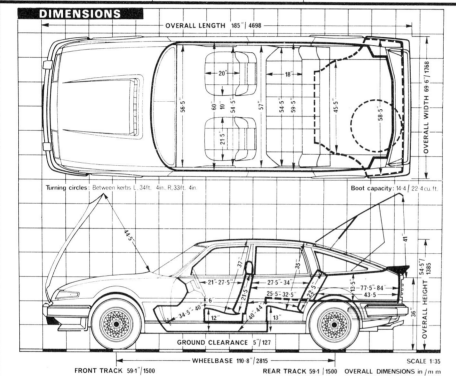

OVERALL LENGTH 185" / 4698
OVERALL WIDTH 69·6" / 1768

Turning circles : Between kerbs L, 34ft. 4in. R, 33ft. 4in.

Boot capacity: 14·4 / 22·4 cu. ft.

GROUND CLEARANCE 5" / 127
OVERALL HEIGHT 54·5" / 1385
WHEELBASE 110·8" / 2815
FRONT TRACK 59·1" / 1500
REAR TRACK 59·1 / 1500
OVERALL DIMENSIONS in / mm
SCALE 1:35

PRICES

Basic	£12,000.00
Special Car Tax	£1,000.00
VAT	£1,950
Total (in GB)	**£14,950.**
Licence	£80.00
Delivery charge (London)	£126.50
Number plates	£20.00
Total on the Road (exc. insurance)	**£15,176.50**

EXTRAS *(inc. VAT)*

Air conditioning	£1,011.13
Electric sunroof	£113.00

*Fitted to test car

TOTAL AS TESTED ON THE ROAD	**£15,176.50**
Insurance	Group 8/OA

SERVICE & PARTS

	Interval	
Change	12,000	24,000
Engine oil	Yes	Yes
Oil filter	Yes	Yes
Gearbox oil	No	Check
Spark plugs	No	Yes
Air cleaner	No	Yes
Total cost	**£58.73**	**£92.12**

(Assuming labour at £17.83/hour inc. VAT)

PARTS COST *(including VAT)*

Brake pads (2 wheels) – front	£51.75
Brake shoes (2 wheels) – rear	£29.44
Exhaust complete	£179.98
Tyre – each (typical)	£139.71
Windscreen	£96.03
Headlamp unit (lens only)	£10.47
Front wing	£85.10
Rear bumper	£41.98

WARRANTY

12 months' unlimited mileage

SPECIFICATION

ENGINE

	Front, rear-wheel drive
Head/block	Al. alloy/al. alloy
Cylinders	8 in 90deg, V dry liners
Main bearings	5
Cooling	Water
Fan	Viscous
Bore, mm (in.)	88.9 (3.50)
Stroke, mm (in.)	71.1 (2.80)
Capacity, cc (in.³)	3,528 (215.0)
Valve gear	Ohv
Camshaft drive	Chain
Compression ratio	9.75-to-1
Ignition	Breakerless
Injection	Lucas L electronic system
Max power	190 bhp (DIN) at 5,280 rpm
Max torque	220 lb. ft. at 4,000 rpm

TRANSMISSION

Type	Five-speed synchromesh
Clutch	Single dry plate

Gear	Ratio	mph/1000rpm
Top	0.792	29.4
4th	1.000	23.3
3rd	1.396	16.7
2nd	2.087	11.1
1st	3.320	7.0
Final drive gear	Hypoid	
Ratio	3.08	

SUSPENSION

Front – location	Independent Mac-Pherson strut
– springs	Coil
– dampers	Telescopic
– anti-roll bar	Yes
Rear – location	Live axle, torque tube, trailing arms, Watts linkage
– springs	Coil
– dampers	Telescopic
– anti-roll bar	No

STEERING

Type	Rack and pinion
Power assistance	Yes
Wheel diameter	16.5×15.5 in.
Turns lock to lock	3.0

BRAKES

Circuits	
Front	10.1 in. dia. ventilated disc
Rear	9.0 in. dia drum
Servo	Vacuum
Handbrake	Centre lever working on rear drums

WHEELS

Type	Cast alloy
Rim width	6½ in. J
Tyres – make	Goodyear NCT
– type	Radial ply tubeless
– size	205/60VR-15
– pressures	F 24, R 26 psi (normal driving)

EQUIPMENT

Battery	12V 66Ah
Alternator	75A
Headlamps	110/230W
Reversing lamp	Standard
Electric fuses	10
Screen wipers	2-speed plus intermittent/flick wipe
Screen washer	Electric
Interior heater	Air blending
Air conditioning	Extra
Interior trim	Cloth seats, nylon headlining
Floor covering	Carpet
Jack	Screw pillar
Jacking points	At each corner
Windscreen	Laminated
Underbody protection	Bitumastic wax zinc coated sills

HOW THE ROVER VITESSE COMPARES

Rover Vitesse   £14,950

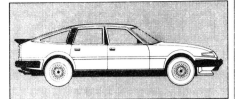

Front engine, rear drive

Capacity
3,528 c.c.

Power
190 bhp (DIN)
at 5,280 rpm

Weight
3,136 lb/1,424 kg

Autotest
12 February 1983

Audi 200T   £14,313

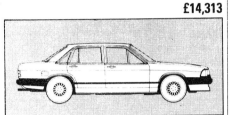

Front engine, front drive

Capacity
2,144 c.c.

Power
170 bhp (DIN)
at 5,300 rpm

Weight
2,856 lb/1,297 kg

Autotest
4 July 1981

BMW 735i   £18,500

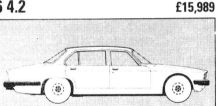

Front engine, rear drive

Capacity
3,453 c.c.

Power
218 bhp (DIN)
at 5,200 rpm

Weight
3,472 lb/1,577 kg

Autotest
22 January 1983

Jaguar XJ6 4.2   £15,989

Front engine, rear drive

Capacity
4,235 c.c.

Power
205 bhp (DIN)
at 5,000 rpm

ght
5 lb/1,760 kg

Autotest
29 December 1979

Mercedes 380SE (A)   £18,800

Front engine, rear drive

Capacity
3,839 c.c.

Power
204 bhp (DIN)
at 5,250 rpm

Weight
3,516 lb/1,595 kg

Autotest
17 July 1982 (380SEC)

Opel Monza S 3.0E   £14,591

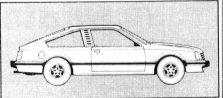

Front engine, rear drive

Capacity
2,968 c.c.

Power
180 bhp (DIN)
at 5,800 rpm

Weight
3,268 lb/1,484 kg

Autotest
14 November 1981

MPH & MPG

Maximum speed (mph)

Opel Monza S 3.0E	133
*Mercedes 380SE (A)	131
Rover Vitesse	130
BMW 735i (A)	129
Jaguar XJ6 4.2 (A)	127
Audi 200 T	125

Acceleration 0-60 (sec)

Audi 200T	7.5
Rover Vitesse	7.6
BMW 735i (A)	7.8
Opel Monza S 3.0E	8.5
*Mercedes 380SE (A)	9.1
Jaguar XJ6 4.2 (A)	10.0

Overall mpg

Opel Monza S 3.0E	23.0
Rover Vitesse	21.8
*Mercedes 380SE (A)	20.0
BMW 735i (A)	19.6
Audi 200 T	19.1
Jaguar XJ6 4.2 (A)	16.8

*Figures for 380SEC (A)

Presently the new super aerodynamic Audi 100 is only available in normally aspirated form, so VAG are still selling the "old" 200T; a car with urgent mid-range acceleration if the lowest top speed of the group. The Quattro (£17,052, 135 mph, 7.3sec and 19.1 mpg) is always worth consideration, especially now it is available with right-hand drive. Of this group, honour for highest top speed belongs to the deceptively fast Opel, which like the Mercedes, was maximum speed tested on the road, ie without the adverse effect of the slight cornering loads found at Millbrook (where the BMW and Rover were tested) at these speeds. The Monza is easily beaten off the line by the front-wheel-drive Audi, the Rover, and the delightfully eager, responsive and mechanically refined BMW, which as the figures show is less than usually hampered by having automatic transmission thanks to its four speeds and top gear lock-up.

The big Rover stands out for its fuel economy and performance. The Jaguar is not so outstanding here, but its sheer weight does assure a high degree of passenger compartment noise refinement.

ON THE ROAD

The XJ6 still rates as the paragon of ride, handling, balance and road noise refinement. It could still do with a little more steering weight, as could the Rover. The BMW, Mercedes and Opel are ideal in this respect. Of the three, the Opel and latest BMW 735i have just the better ride, but both are apt to tail slide in *extremis* – the Opel also has perhaps the most cornering roll. By contrast the Vitesse rolls very little, and is very reluctant to be provoked into oversteer – in fact under most extreme cornering conditions pronounced understeer is likely to be the sole characteristic encountered, just as it will be on the Audi, which considering 170 bhp is being transmitted through the front wheels rates tolerably well for its wet weather

traction. Main drawback with the 200T is road noise and its ride sensitivity to minor unevenesses. Within the physical restraints imposed on them Rover chassis engineers have done a good job for in spite of the understeer, it is great fun to drive. Not surprisingly it falls some way short of the ride sophistication found in the immediate competition – but on the plus side has very crisp below-limit handling response. All stop well, but where braking on slippery surfaces is concerned the BMW has a clear advantage since ABS anti-lock is fitted as standard.

In heating and ventilation all six work well, though the twin water valve heater in the Mercedes takes longer to respond than the air blending systems in the rest.

SIZE & SPACE

Legroom front/rear (in.)

(seats fully back)

BMW 735i (A)	42/40
Mercedes 380SE	42/40
Rover Vitesse	40/40
Audi 200T	42/37
Jaguar XJ 4.2	39/38.5
Opel Monza S 3.0E	30/36

Penalty for the Monza's relatively short wheelbase and low roof line is a relative lack of leg and head room in the rear. With some front seat adjustments it can provide tolerable accomodation for four. The BMW and Mercedes are very generously proportioned inside, and like the Audi have large luggage carrying capacities.

Most versatile proposition (after the three-door Opel) is clearly the Rover. It too lacks sufficient headroom for the really tall but provides excellent accomodation for four and a really decent load area with the rear seats folded down.

VERDICT

It's horses for courses. Those that demand the ultimate combination of ride, handling and refinement must seriously consider the Jaguar. Though costly, the BMW has ABS brakes as standard, a wonderful engine, better handling and ride than previous 735is and considerably more mid-range performance than the equally costly Mercedes. There is something very exciting about the way the 200T surges forward in the mid range, yet both the Opel and Rover provide a better blend of performance and economy – and the latter has much more load carrying versatility than the rest. Enthusiastic drivers are likely to relish the fairly stiffly sprung Rover's handling and acceleration response, if not some slightly agricultural aspects of its ride (and the lacklustre gearchange). It may lack the overall sophistication of some of its peers, yet we ended up liking the car almost for this very reason. It has a distinctly "animal" character all of its own.

12,000 Miles On

QUESTIONABLE QUALITY CONTROL

With excessive wind noise, twitchy steering and sloppy dampers, our staff Rover 3500 SE is not a good example of its kind — and niggling faults have marred its record. Anthony Curtis reports

WITH ITS Ferrari shape, hatchback practicality, impressive roadholding and excellent performance, the Rover 3500 'SD1' excited high hopes when it was first introduced in 1976. Produced in a brand new purpose-built factory at Solihull, its potential sales were well in excess of 100,000 a year, and it seemed to have in its favour every factor needed to make it an outstanding success.

Every factor save one, perhaps, and that was the most important of all: the human factor. For production of the Rover became one of those sad and all-too-British tales of troubled labour relations and stop-go-manufacture. Thus in 1977, the first full year of its production, only 25,649 cars were built altogether. During that same year, 202,754 examples were produced of the Audi 100, a major rival in the executive express market.

Then the fuel crisis finally bit into the market for large European cars, and quality inevitably deteriorated with the wrangles and assembly-line hiccups,

until the Rover range — by then augmented with the six-cylinder 2300 and 2600 models — almost symbolised the parlous state into which BL fell during the late seventies.

Since then, happily, the fortunes of BL have improved remarkably, and those of the Rover range along with them. The market for executive models revived a little, and the quality of the car improved greatly after production was transferred to Cowley. Public recognition of this improvement was then consolidated by the introduction at the beginning of last year of an updated range, including a new 2000 model, which was thus given significantly more appeal. The still newer and sporting Vitesse model has enhanced this appeal still further, as has the success of the racing Rovers in the Trimoco British Saloon Car Championship. As a result, production rose to 32,885 cars last year, and secondhand values have soared.

It was partly in anticipation of this success, but partly to evaluate the 'Mk

2' version of the Rover — plus all the other modifications instituted over the years — that we decided to subject another example to long-term test. (Regular readers may remember our long term report on an early 3500, *Motor* November 27, 1976). The budget would have stretched to a Vanden Plas car, perhaps the most modified and certainly the best equipped in the range with its trip computer and other luxuries. However, trip computers leave me cold, so I settled for a 3500 SE with manual transmission and haven't much regretted the choice, despite its poor AM radio, since the SE has plenty of walnut and luxury anyway.

In common with all 3500s, then, my car has the superb Rover light-alloy V8 engine, still producing 155 bhp at 5,250 rpm and a hefty 198 lb ft of torque at 2,500 rpm, and little modified since its first adoption for the SD1 in 1976. It drives through a five-speed manual gearbox which has always had very high ratios, that of fifth being higher still (from the 1981 model year) when it was changed to give 29.7 mph/1,000 rpm instead of 28.1 mph/1,000 rpm. From this gearbox the drive passes to the live rear axle with its Spen King arrangement of a torque

tube and radius arms for longitudinal location, and a Watts linkage for transverse location. As on the 2600 S and Vanden Plas models, constant-rate springs work in conjunction with self-levelling spring/damper units. As before, there is a MacPherson strut suspension system at the front with coil springs and an anti-roll bar, working in conjunction with rack and pinion steering, now power-assisted on all but the 2000 and 2300 models.

Externally, Mk 2 cars are easily distinguished from their predecessors — by a spoiler at the front, added to improve high-speed stability, and at the rear by the downward enlargement of the tailgate window. Inside, the main difference, apart from more luxurious trim, lies in the larger and more elaborate instrument pod with 'quartic' dials for the speedometer and rev-counter.

ON DELIVERY

Following our established practice, pursued whenever the accountants will let us, my 3500 SE, finished in zircon blue, was bought rather than borrowed and arrived in the middle of June last year. It was supplied with the wrong hand-

some wind noise, but otherwise found the car very quiet and refined. The first 'free' (£9.35 for lubricants) 1,000-mile service was competently carried out by University Motors at Epsom.

LIFE WITH THE 3500 SE

For seasons that will gradually emerge, I view my own car with considerably less enthusiasm than I do its kind as a whole. Rover's quality control obviously still has some way to go — or at least, it did when my car was built — and experiences with various road test cars have clearly shown that PJH 926X must lie right at the bottom end of the tolerance limits in various important respects such as wind noise and steering feel. In addition, although it has not so far let me down completely (and it has now covered nearly 18,000 miles) it has suffered from a host of niggling faults.

I have nothing but praise, though, for the torquey effortlessness and unruffled smoothness of its engine. The Rover 3500 is by any standards a respectably brisk car, and our recent performance test proved *Motor*'s example to be well up to par in maximum speed — attaining nearly 122 mph at Mill-

book, thus leaving me, as already described in a Running Report (*Motor*, November 20, 1982) to work out on my own rules for running in — which were to stick to 3,000 rpm for the first 1,000 miles and progressively raise the rev-limit thereafter. These proved rather more sensible than the instructions in the correct handbook, which, when it arrived a few days later, the recommendations of which included a suggested maximum speed, for the first 500 miles, of 45 mph — equivalent to little more than 1,500 rpm in top.

The car had no obvious faults or blemishes, however, except for a loose plastic surround to the driver's door locking button. During that initial running-in phase, I began to notice a gearbox whine in second and third and

imum speed is over 100 mph) on a fast cross-country run on twisty roads. But I've learned both to tolerate and to exploit the car's long-legged stride: even in heavy urban traffic it's surprising how often it is possible to waft gently along in that very high top. I don't dislike the gearchange either, despite its slightly heavy and notchy action, and although it continues to whine in second and third, a little filter in my head has decided to tune out this particular sound so that I now seldom notice it.

Another great virtue of the car, as far as I am concerned, is its versatility — though I still feel that the tailgates of all hatchbacks ought to extend down to the floors of the luggage compartments they enclose to eliminate any sill over which luggage has to be lifted. Nevertheless, despite its high rear lip, the Rover's fifth door, forward-folding rear seats and roomy luggage compartment with its removable cover have time and time again proved useful for the conveyance of a wide selection of heavy or bulky objects, ranging from furniture to boat bits of various sorts.

My feelings about the Rover's seating arrangements and driving position are more neutral. For a car that is pretty

Our staff example corners and handles well, though with twitchy steering and sloppy dampers it is less fun to drive than it should be

brook — and in acceleration away from the lights, its 0-60 mph time being 9.2 sec. These figures are almost identical to those obtained from the V8 S which we tested in 1980.

The objective performance tests, however, also show that the acceleration of my car is noticeably poorer in fourth gear, and (as would be expected) still more inferior in its higher fifth, recording, for example, a 30-50 mph time in this ratio of 13.7 sec compared to the 10.7 sec of the V8 S. Subjectively, though, I've never noticed any deficiency, and am often impressed by the way in which the engine will pull smoothly and strongly from low rpm.

This is in spite of the fact that I always used to consider the gearing of the 3500 to be a good deal too high. Even now, I may hardly use a gear higher than third (in which the max-

large — it's over 15 ft long — its front-seat legroom is distinctly mediocre by the standards of today. This deficiency is compounded by a knees-up driving position which I always find odd after driving another car, and by a seat which lacks a height adjustment. It does have an adjustable lumbar support, but it must have been designed around an underslung mannikin, for it is located much nearer to my bottom than to the small of my back. Despite all this, the feeling of oddness wears off after a few minutes and I accumulate no aches or pains after a long journey.

I don't like the non-circular steering wheel, but am indifferent to the new instrument display, though I find I can see all its dials without difficulty.

I am very much less tolerant, however, of the very high level of wind noise from which the car has always suffered, and which makes it markedly less refined at high speeds than such rivals as 5-Series BMWs. Poor sealing around the door frames seems to be the principal cause, and this was not improved by a blow to the nearside external mirror — received at an early stage in the car's life when it was parked in a narrow Paris street — which slightly distorted the frame of the door to which it was attached. Naturally I complained about the problem to the dealers then handling the car: University Motors of Epsom. But although the temporary increase in noise level was eliminated by the necessary repairs to mirror and door, no reduction in the basic volume of hissing and rustling noises was achieved.

It wasn't in order to compete with this high noise level that I decided to have fitted to the car a complex Sharp audio system involving a graphic equaliser and separate amplifiers for front and rear speakers. It was simply that the original-equipment AM radio was hopeless, though its performance wasn't helped by a poor contact in the electrically-operated aerial. But the Sharp system certainly has bags of power and reproduces music with admirable accuracy when the cassette player is used. Its radio reception, however, is mediocre, thougt the aerial may perhaps be partly to blame.

Had the car been almost any example other than my own particular one, the excessive wind noise would almost certainly have been at least partially redeemed, from a driving pleasure

<table>
<tr><td colspan="2" align="center">**MOTOR LONG TERM TEST**</td></tr>
<tr><td colspan="2" align="center">**ROVER 3500 SE**</td></tr>
<tr><td>Total mileage: **12,868**</td><td>Value now: **£8,800**</td></tr>
<tr><td>When acquired: **June, 1982**</td><td>Overall mpg: **19.8**</td></tr>
<tr><td>Price when new: **£12,546**</td><td>Days off road: **none**</td></tr>
<tr><td>Price now: **£12,496**</td><td>Extra visits to dealer: **two**</td></tr>
</table>

Make: Rover　　　　　　　　　**Model:** 3500 SE
Maker: Austin Rover Group Limited, Canley Road, Canley, Coventry, CV5 6QX. **Tel:** 0203 70111
Price: £10,030.00 Basic plus £835.83 Car Tax plus £1,629.87 VAT equals £12,495.70

 excellent good average poor bad

point of view, by the inherent excellence of the handling and roadholding. Certainly my own car clings well to the road, and corners in a responsive and progressive way with mild understeer. Lifting off in mid-bend induces little change in attitude, even when pressing on. When turning right from a standstill, it is quite difficult *not* to lift and spin the inside rear wheel momentarily, but for left-hand starts and in most other circumstances — including the wet — the tail stays firmly glued to the road unless provoked with a lot of throttle in a low gear.

But the pleasure which might otherwise be derived from exploiting these admirable characteristics, is significantly blunted by two major deficiences. By far the worst of these is the poor quality of the power steering, which is not merely totally lacking in 'feel', failing to transmit the right messages to the driver, but actually generates some false messages of its own, at times, when it causes the wheel to twitch in ones hands when the car is cornering steadily on a smooth surface and there is no reason for such perturbations. In fast, sweeping bends and during motorway cruising, my car can thus be distinctly uncomfortable to drive. Several times I have stopped to check

the pressures of the front tyres convinced of some major imbalance or partial deflation, only to find nothing wrong in this department.

This first weakness is compounded by the second: the uncharacteristic way in which my particular car tends to lurch rather rapidly into corners, suggesting inadequate damping of roll movements. By the high standards normally set by good examples of the Rover breed, my car is therefore a little vague and untidy when driven fast on a twisty road.

These faults became apparent at an early stage in the car's life, but for a time I endured them without complaint, telling myself that I was being too fussy. Then I drove our road test Diesel Turbo model and found it so much more taut and responsive than my own car — so much more like the SD1 Rovers I had driven in the past, in fact — that my dissatisfaction returned. It was endorsed when I paid a visit to BL Technology at Gaydon to learn about their impressive ECV3 experimental car. There, an engineer test-drove my car, diagnosed a sticking valve in the power steering system and confirmed the below-par condition of (at under 8,000 miles) the dampers. Few dealers have the know-how to

deal effectively with relatively subtle faults of this sort, in my experience, but nevertheless I considered it my duty to have them put right through normal channels, if at all possible, and therefore asked University Motors of Epsom to investigate. Unfortunately, my gloomy prognostications were confirmed: according to their tests, no fault could be found either with the power steering system or the dampers. However, I have now decided to take up an offer made some time ago through Austin Rover's Public Relations Department to put right the wind noise as well as the power steering system and the dampers. I will report on the results in due course.

RELIABILITY

Although my car has not yet let me down completely, it has come pretty close to it on one or two occasions, and has suffered from a whole range of niggling minor faults and failures. By the time it had covered 5,000 miles, for example, these included a tailgate that leaked water in the rain, a flickering front brake pad wear warning light, a bad contact in the electric aerial, a failed temperature gauge light, a clonk in the rear suspension when entering left-hand bends, appalling dipped headlamp beams, and a reluctance on the part of the starter motor to crank the engine on the first turn of the key. The leaking tailgate was cured under warranty by Mann Egerton in Wallington and has remained watertight, the temperature gauge light bulb was successfully replaced, the aerial performance improved, albeit only temporarily, and the clonk in the rear suspension, which persisted for quite a time, has now gone away of its own accord.

But the flickering brake pad wear warning light proved no fault: the front brake pads were indeed worn. Since the light first began to flicker at well under 5,000 miles, and since I'd hardly done any fast motoring in the car at the time, I regarded such a short pad life as being quite unacceptable. Austin Rover now admit that some brake pads made at that time were manufactured to a "faulty materials specification". Certainly the second set of pads lasted a good deal longer, but brake performance isn't one of the car's strongest

points, severe judder being common in moderate usage.

I was even less pleased by the way in which the headlamp problem was finally resolved. The appalling poor dipped beams were found to be caused by the fact that the car was 'cross-eyed': it had the correct left-hand dip headlamp on one side, but a Continental right-hand dip unit on the other. When I pointed this out to the receptionist at University Motors, I was told that it couldn't be replaced under warranty, because although it was the wrong unit, there was nothing wrong with it! Rather than argue this somewhat confused piece of philosophy, I asked for the faulty headlamp unit to be replaced, regardless of any warranty considerations — and so it was, at a cost of over £60.

As to the starting problem, this maddening fault persists to this day. I turn the key and there is a distant click as if the solenoid had been energised, but the starter motor fails to turn. Often I have to turn the key back and forth several times before the starter motor condescends to spring into life and fire up the engine.

During the next 3,000 miles further persistent problems revealed themselves: the central locking system failed for the first of several times and the coolant level warning light began to flicker, even though there was no obvious loss of water and the level in the small plastic header tank was either correct or only slightly below the mark. This fault persisted for several thousand miles, only disappearing after University Motors' second or third attempt to cure it. The central locking system, though, continues to give trouble, being inoperative as I write, the car having now covered 17,900 miles. It has its own special fuse, somewhere under the luggage compartment, which doesn't seem to be man enough for the job. And just as the central locking system began to play up, the electrically operated aerial refused to raise or lower itself, though this fault was cured and has not recurred.

I was all set to record another fault which I thought I had encount when the car had covered just un.. ..r 9,000 miles and the nearside rear tyre slowly flattened itself having picked up a small piece of metal on the Kingston By-Pass. So I looked for the jacking points, where they are usually to be

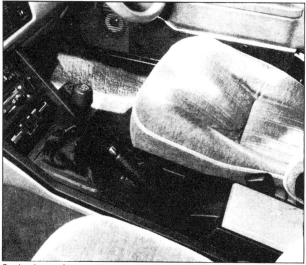
Barely adequate front-seat legroom and a knees up driving position are not the most endearing features of the Rover's packaging

Superb powerhouse: the light alloy V8 gives effortless performance

The fold-forward rear seat and roomy luggage compartment, seen here with its cover removed, has proved invaluable for the transport of bulky objects of all sorts

found, in the sills of the car, following the instructions of the handbook which says only that "jacking points are provided for each side of the vehicle". And (so I thought) I found them. the only problem was that each one was partially blocked by a sheet of metal, as if some last-stage robot had failed to punch the cut-outs essential to make them usable. Accordingly, I had no option but to call the AA for help, and when a man with a trolley jack arrived, the wheel was swiftly changed.

All this will no doubt prove a big laugh to SD1 Rover owners of long standing, but only in the last few days have I learned that the jacking points are located in the front and rear bumpers. But even armed with this esoteric piece of knowledge, I still find the handbook drawing vague and ambiguous.

A further problem revealed itself at around 11,000 miles towards the end of February during that long period of wet weather which blanketed the whole of Europe for the first part of the year. I had left the car at Heathrow Airport for a few days, and on returning to it, found that while the starter motor ‌er the usual several twists of the ‌‌‌y) would happily and vigorously turn the engine over, it wouldn't start. There was nothing obvious amiss under the bonnet, but a marked absence of spark seemed to be the problem — presumably because of the dampness, though one would hardly expect a modern (electronic) ignition system to suffer in this way. Eventually, with the throttle floored and after several minutes of churning, one cylinder began to fire, then another, until the engine finally became self-sustaining. I expected the 20-mile run home to dry everything out satisfactorily, but the weather still being wet, I encountered the same problem the next day — and it persisted for some weeks. Spraying some WD40 on the distributor and ignition leads would usually cure it, though, confirming my belief that dampness was the cause. I am still amazed and disgusted that a modern car can suffer from such a fault; it ‌ ‌n't recurred, but then, the weather ‌‌‌been pretty dry for the last couple of months.

And with the warmth that has recently come to Britain along with the dryness, yet another fault has been encountered, though strictly speaking it should be covered in my next report, because it did not occur until some 14,500 miles had been covered. At first I thought it was a recurrence of the cooling system problems, for during a short spell of warm weather in early May the needle of the water temperature gauge began to hover perilously close to the red zone. Then I noticed that the fuel gauge was over-reading by about 50 per cent, as was the oil pressure gauge. My conclusion, therefore, is that it is not the engine itself which overheats in warm weather, but some instrument voltage control unit buried in the bowels of the facia.

SERVICING

★
★ As is so often the case with our staff cars, my Rover was bought from a dealer (Julians of Reading) in another part of the country, so the first service and all warranty work had to be carried out by garages other than the original selling agent.

But dealers local to our Sutton offices showed no reluctance to carry out such work, and as already mentioned, the first, 1,000-mile service was competently performed by University Motors of Epsom.

A recall notice concerning the steering column (which subsequently proved to be irrelevant to my car) provided the opportunity to try out another garage in the Austin Rover network, so the car was taken to Mann Egerton in Wallington. There the pad wear problem was resolved, the faulty temperature gauge light replaced, the leaking tailgate repaired and the headlamp fault diagnosed (but no spare units were in stock at the time).

However, I was not impressed to find the rear wiper blade missing immediately after this work had, been carried out, nor did this garage ever contact me, as they said they would, to say that a replacement headlamp unit had been received. Apart from their aberration about the replacement of that headlamp unit, University Motors of Epsom, who have carried out all other work on the car, proved competent, knowledgeable and helpful.

COSTS

★★
★★ For a large, roomy car with plenty of performance, my Rover 3500 SE has not proved expensive to run, I feel. In view of the considerable extent to which that performance has been used, I can't complain about the 19.8 mpg it has returned, and I've noticed that a number of other members of Motor's staff, with gentler driving habits than mine, have regularly recorded over 20 mpg.

Its maintenance requirements are reasonable, too. After that first 1,000 service no attention is required until a major service at 12,000 miles (or after one year) which cost £125.03. Another visit to the garage cost £152.13, but I have only included £65 of this in the cost analysis to take account of the headlamp replacement (I shouldn't have been charged, of course, but the unit cost £61.50 and I've added a little for labour) since the total sum included replacement of the dinged door mirror and attention to the slightly bent door frame.

The tyre wear has also been reasonable, in my view. The front tyres still have 5mm left of their initial 8mm of tread, but the original (offside) rear tyre is down to 3mm and will soon have to be swopped over with the spare. Since the other rear tyre (replaced after the puncture) is little worn, this should keep the car on the road for another 18,000 miles.

SECOND OPINION

HAVING DRIVEN Tony Curtis's Rover several times, I fully endorse his opinion that while it remains a very pleasant car, it isn't as good as Rovers can be. Whenever I get into it I am initially surprised by the strange performance of the steering, but I find that the chassis is good enough for that — and the initially large and sudden amount of roll when entering a bend rapidly — to be an irritation rather than a major cause of annoyance.

What I would find hard to accept in everyday driving is the wind roar even

COSTS

PETROL	649 gallons at £1.80 per gallon	1,168.20
OIL	between services, 5 litres at £1.70 per litre	8.50
SERVICING	at 947 miles	9.35
	at 12,694 miles	152.13
REPAIRS	at 8,500 miles replacement of faulty headlamp	65.00
TYRES	50 per cent worn overall: £99.13 per tyre	198.26
ROAD FUND LICENCE	for 12 months	85.00
TOTAL		
for 12,868 miles		£1,686.44
BASIC COST PER MILE		13.1p

PERFORMANCE

WEATHER CONDITIONS

Wind	0-5 mph
Temperature	57°F/13.9°C
Barometer	29.7 in Hg
Surface	Dry tarmacadam

MAXIMUM SPEEDS

	mph	mph
	R/T car	L/T car
Banked circuit	122.0	121.7
Terminal Speeds:		
at ¼ mile	81	84
at kilomtre	103	105

Speeds in gears (at 6,000 rpm):
1st	42	42
2nd	67	67
3rd	101	101

ACCELERATION FROM REST

mph	sec	sec
0-30	3.1	3.2
0-40	4.9	4.8
0-50	6.9	6.7
0-60	9.1	9.2
0-70	12.7	12.0
0-80	16.2	15.5
0-90	20.	19.1
0-100	28.3	27.0
Stand'g ¼	16.6	16.9
Stand'g km	30.8	31.1

ACCELERATION IN TOP

mph	sec	sec
20-40	11.7	16.1
30-50	10.7	13.7
40-60	10.7	13.9
50-70	10.i	14.0
60-80	11.5	15.0
70-90	13.5	18.5
80-100	17.7	—

ACCELERATION IN 4TH

mph	sec	sec
20-40	8.5	9.8
30-50	7.7	8.8
40-60	7.5	8.8
50-70	7.6	8.6
60-80	8.4	9.2

70-90	9.8	11.0
80-100	12.3	14.4

FUEL CONSUMPTION

	R/T	L/T
Touring*	23.6	24.1
Overall	18.9 mpg	19.8 mpg
Govt tests	16.2 mpg (urban)	
	36.3 mpg (56 mph)	
	28.9 mpg (75 mph)	
Fuel grade	97 octane	
	4 star rating	
Tank capacity	14.5 galls	
	66 litres	
Max range	342 miles	
	551 km	
Test distance	2,475 miles 12,868 miles	

*An estimated fuel consumption computed from the theoretical consumption at a steady speed midway between 30 mph and the car's maximum, less a 5 per cent allowance for acceleration.

NOISE

	R/T	L/T
	dBA	dBA
30 mph	61	65
50 mph	65	70
70 mph	72	74
Maximum†	80	80·5

†Peak noise level under full-throttle acceleration in 2nd

SPEEDOMETER (mph)

Speedo	30 40 50 60 70 80 90 100
True mph	33 43 53 63 72.5 82.5 92.5 102.5
Distance recorder: 3 per cent slow	

WEIGHT

	cwt	kg
Unladen weight*	26.8	1,360
Weight as tested	30.5	1,548

*with fuel for approx 50 miles

Performance tests carried out by Motor's staff at the Motor Industry Research Association proving ground, Lindley.

Test Data: World Copyright reserved. No reproduction in whole or part without written permission.

THE RIVALS

Included below is comparative information on the BMW 528i, Ford Granada 2.8i, Mercedes 280E, Saab 900 Turbo 4-dr and Talbot Tagora SX.

PERFORMANCE	Rover†	BMW	Ford	Mercedes††	Saab	Talbot
Max speed, mph	122.0	129.8	117.5	125e	120.8	115.8
Max in 4th	—	—	—	—	110	116
Max in 3rd	101	98	98	90	79	80
2nd	67	62	68	55	53	53
1st	42	36	37	33	30	30
0-60 mph, secs	9.1	7.7	9.0	9.5	8.9	8.3
30-50 mph in 4th, secs	7.7	8.6	10.1	4.5¹	7.5	7.3
50-70 mph in top, secs	10.7	12.	‡	ə	†	‡‡
Weight, cwt	27.0	26.0	26.3	30.2	23.8	25.8
Turning circle, ft*	31.1	32.3	32.2	32.5	31.4	32.3
50ft circle, turns	0.85	1.2	0.7	0.95	1.2	1.15
Boot capacity, cu.ft.	12.7	13.2	13.2	14.2	14.5	15.1

*mean of left and right †Figures for Rovers V8 s ‡ Automatic
¹in kickdown for automatic ᵉestimated

COSTS AND SERVICE	Rover	BMW	Ford	Mercedes	Saab	Talbot
Price, inc VAT & tax, £	12,496	13,575	11,175	13,600	11,545	11,445
Insurance group	7	8	7	8	8	6
Overall mpg	18.9	21.6	20.5	17.2	21.0	17.5
Touring mpg	23.6	—	—	—	—	21.1
Fuel grade (stars)	4	4	4	4	4	4
Tank capacity, gals	14.5	15.4	14.3	17.6	13.9	15.6
Service interval, miles	12,000	*	6,000	12,000	10,000	10,000
No of dealers	1,550	148	1,200	103	159	530
Recom service time in hours for 12,000 miles	2.75	**	3.6	4.2	2.75	

*determined by BMW Automatic Service Indicator
**depends upon findings of BMW Automatic Service Indicator

at relatively modest cruising speeds, and I agree that this is a fault on this particular car rather than a general design defect.

When I drove the car last, it had covered nearly 18,000 miles, and I must say that it seems to have stood the test of time pretty well, though there are one or two items of interior trim (such as the door-lock buttons) that are by no means perfect.

I think it's a pity that Rover don't fit the suspension/tyre package of the Vitesse to all the more powerful versions of the car, as the very small penalty in ride quality is compensated substantially by improved handling. Having said that, even this uncharacteristically twitchy example of the SE is still a match for its opposition on a twisty road.

You will probably have gathered by now that I am enthusiastic about Rovers. I like them despite a number of things which are inherently quite bad about them: the forward visibility in tight spaces, the instruments, the relatively mean amount of accommodation supplied in what is a fairly big car, and some aspects of interior trim finish. They have a tremendous amount of character, and I for one will be very sad when this model, and its magnificent V8 engine, is eventually replaced by something which will no doubt be more efficient and more competent.

Peter Dron

MANUFACTURER'S COMMENT

We are pleased that Tony Curtis has found Rover's major design objectives — to provide an excellent combination of performance, refinement, handling and roadholding — have been amply fulfilled by this particular example. Additionally, it is noteworthy that he has found the running costs reasonable in relation to the usage, which we suspect has been more than a little on the hard side and therefore probably not entirely typical.

This particular car was built at Solihull and Tony rightly acknowledges that the quality of the Rover generally has improved greatly following its transfer to Cowley. Certainly the Rover of today is unlikely to suffer from the small and niggling problems he has reported.

On the question of wind noise, clearly the damaged door panel will have exacerbated the situation. However, this is an area where quite small variations in tolerance can make a deal of difference and where the correct adjustment or profile of the door, to which we have been devoting significant attention at Cowley, is important in achieving an optimum condition. We have also done some additional development work on the door seals themselves and new Rovers are fitted with a modified seal which makes a further contribution towards lower wind noise levels.

Since assembly commenced at Cowley, levels of road and water ingress testing have been increased to the point where every car built is now subject to both as a matter of course. Every car is also subject to a computerised electrical check-up to ensure the integrity of the electrical circuitry at the time the car leaves the factory. On the subject of electrical circuitry, we were dissatisfied with the reliability performance of the central door lock mechanism. As a result we have specified a completely different system from a new supplier and will continue to be intolerant of any supplier who fails to meet agreed performance and reliability criteria. A service bulletin was issued to dealers last November detailing the action required to rectify the original system when problems were being experienced.

As to brake pad wear, we were not satisfied with pad life, particularly in city driving, and did change to a more durable material — and a different supplier — early in the life of the 1982 model year Rovers.

Clearly it is not possible to comment with any certainty upon the criticisms made of the steering and 'inadequate damping' on this particular car until we have had the opportunity to examine it. However the characteristics described are not recognised by us — or indeed by you — as generally applying to the model. We shall, at the same time, look into the starting difficulties.

We accept the point about the jacking instructions. Although the illustrations show both towing eye and exhaust pipe, the accompanying text is not as clear as it might be. We will revise it as quickly as possible.

We can understand Tony Curtis's exasperation at the refusal of the dealer to replace the wrongly fitted continental headlamp unit. Clearly if a part on a new vehicle is wrongly specified it should be changed free of charge by the dealer.

READER FEEDBACK

Quite a few readers responded to our requests for information on their experiences with their Rovers, but only 26 of the questionnaires received referred to the 'Mk 2' 3500 SE introduced at the beginning of 1982. The average age of the cars in this sample was seven months, the average mileage covered 12,000, and as might be expected, 73 per cent were company-owned, while a whopping 96 per cent were serviced by the manufacturer's agent.

As might be expected, too, in the general evaluation of the car such characteristics as cruising ability and boot space were awarded high scores (9.8 out of 10 and 8.0 respectively). More surprisingly — to me at any rate — some other features of the car, including its lights and heating system, also scored highly.

Unfortunately the survey also revealed a poor reliability record, confirming my belief that Austin Rover quality control still leaves a good deal to be desired. The average number of days off the road was 8.7, for instance — compared with 1.1 for the Sierra upon which we recently reported (Motor, July 2). Electrical faults were the biggest single source of complaint, though in many cases inessentials were involved, the radio aerial and central locking system being (as for my car, again) two major culprits. Quite a number of owners complained, as I did, of poor brake pad wear life.

In view of all this, it is not surprising that when asked if they would buy another example, 62 per cent of owners said 'no' or that they were not sure.

Owners' ratings*

Acceleration	7.8
Cruising ability	9.8
Steering	7.4
Roadholding	7.6
Handling	7.5
Braking	6.7
Gearchange	7.1
Clutch action	7.0
Gear ratios	7.5
Ride comfort	6.8
Seat comfort	6.7
Driving position	6.8
Heating	8.3
Ventilation	7.0
Noise at 70 mph	7.2
Instruments	6.2
Minor controls	6.4
Fuel consumption	5.5
Tyre wear	6.9
Visibility	5.6
Lights	9.0
Boot space	8.0
Reliability	5.7
Paintwork	5.6
Rusting	7.0
Styling	7.8

*Owners were asked to rate from "Excellent" to "Bad". The scores are based on giving "Excellent" 10, "Good" 7, "Average" 4, "Poor" 2 and "Bad" 0.

Faults

Number of owners having at least one with:

Engine	58

Transmission	23
Steering, suspension	46
Brakes	54
Electrical	77
Body, paint, trim	62
Fittings	46
Instruments	27

Specific faults mentioned included: carburettor and/or auto-choke problems (5); coolant leaks (2); starting difficulties (2); suspension clonks (5); and brake pad or disc replacement (10). The radio aerial (10) and central locking system (8) were amongst the principal causes of electric trouble, and in addition 12 owners complained about the ease with which the paint work chipped. On average each owner mentioned 6.0 faults.

Time off the road (days)

None	27
½/1 day	—
2/3 days	19
4/6 days	15
10/11 days	12
17/20 days	15
28+ days	12

Average number of days off road 8.7

Servicing by manufacturer's agent

Good	
Fair	
Bad	8

Warranty work

None	—
At least some	100

Satisfied with warranty work?

Yes	42
No/not wholly	58

Would you buy another Rover?

Yes	38
No/not sure	62

CONCLUSIONS

In the bad old days — as far as car manufacturing is concerned — of the Sixties and Seventies, people used to refer to 'Friday' cars made when concentration was flagging on the assembly line — the cars with sandwiches built into their box sections, which broke down repeatedly during the first few hundred miles of their existence. With its numerous detail faults quite clear to me that my own Rover today's equivalent of a 'Friday' car. In a way, though — and this is not meant as sarcasm — its service record does confirm the big improvements in quality control made by Austin Rover during the past few years, since not only is the car as a whole basically sound, but some of the things I have categorised as 'faults' would hardly be noticed by quite a few less demanding owners.

Unlike most car owners, though, I'm often able to drive several examples of a given model in the course of a year or so, and thus am given unusual opportunities to make comparisons. Without those opportunities, I might have been able to dismiss the high wind noise, twitchy steering and lurchy cornering of my car as being the typical and relatively unimportant faults of an ageing design. But having driven several other Rovers I know better: I know that when the current model is correctly assembled, it's still a match for the finest rival cars in the world — as our recent Rover Vitesse versus BMW 528i attests.

The moral, then, is that in the motor industry few things are more important than quality control, and that at the time my car was built Austin Rover hadn't quite got it right.

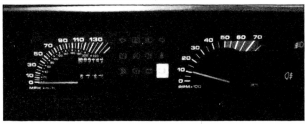

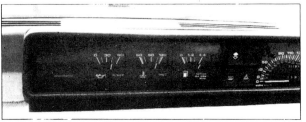

Above left: The brake pad wear warning light wasn't crying wolf — the pads *were* worn out, but at less than 5,000 miles

Left: In hot weather the oil pressure gauge, temperature gauge and fuel gauge tend to over-read simultaneously